ON HEROIN

America, capitalism, and the search for meaning

BRIAN FRANCIS CULKIN

Published by Kindle Direct Publishing.
Cover design by Carlo Parodi © 2019.
Other books by Brian Francis Culkin include Postscript on Boxing, The Meaning of Trump, Conversations on Gentrification, There is No Such Things as Boston, and Spontaneous Reflections.
ISBN: 9781791602482

*I just happen to think that there are times in our lives when we have
to be carried along by the river of events, as if we didn't have the
strength to resist, but then, there comes a point when we suddenly
realize that the river has started to flow in our favor, no one else has
noticed, but we have, anyone else watching will think we are about
to go under, and yet our navigational skills have never been better.*[1]

Jose Saramago, The Cave

to the addicts of Planet Earth and their families ...

Table of Contents

Introduction: From San Francisco to Donald Trump

> *Freedom will prove to have been merely an interlude. Freedom is felt when passing from one way of living to another — until this too turns out to be a form of coercion. Then, liberation gives way to renewed subjugation.*[2]
>
> — *Byung Chul Han*

If you want to see the endgame of neoliberal globalization, perhaps it is best to simply go to the city of San Francisco and patiently observe your surroundings: a cutting-edge tech community, a world class urban economy, and what can only seem a limitless marketplace of self-development services, products, and therapies that cater to every whim of individualized spiritual growth and the optimization of biological health.

But, it is not just these instances of privilege and luxury that define contemporary living in San Francisco. There is also an exploding homeless population, an out of control housing crisis, while nearly all of the various neighborhoods that once housed San Francisco's substantial working and middle class population — not to mention the historically important intellectual and artistic tradition of this city — have been progressively lost over the past twenty years by an influx of tech companies, over-development, and a demographic reconstitution that has seen the city's population transform into a fragmented collection of young cognitive professionals; or, Yuppies as they are usually called.

But what is perhaps most fascinating about this contemporary rearrangement of San Francisco's social substance is the strange fact that as these same young urban professionals are casually walking by a burgeoning homeless population on their way to work, they can quite impressively explain the nuances of white privilege, they can recite with some theoretical accuracy the history of patriarchy within American capitalism, and many of them engage in various consciousness raising activities such as yoga, meditation, even micro-dosing LSD[3] so they can be more spiritually aware and productive in their work.

This weird combination is what you could aptly call the "San Francisification" of American culture, a new social vibration made visible by the emergence of a particular subjectivity that is unique to the operation of late capitalism: in their self-perception these young professionals are part of the "resistance" fighting the good fight, they are the political agents actively breaking all ties with all historical systems of oppression through their various practices of radical innovation and individual creativity — when in actuality they could very well be the emerging symbol of the new model of global capitalism that is now relentlessly undermining *global* life, culture, and community in the 21st century.

In many ways, the "Trumpification" of the other half of American culture directly responds to this very same "San Franciscification." But, this new brand of pseudo-populism and racist nationalism signified by Donald Trump and his followers responds to such rhetorical hypocrisy and ideological blindness — not with honesty and a new kind of universal political discourse — but with reactionary outbursts and digital rage.

To distill what we are bearing witness to right now in American culture and politics is essentially a back and forth between two failed systems and visions for 21st century America: the "San Francisco" vision (technologically mediated neoliberalism with empty gestures of social justice) and the "Trump" vision (nationalist authoritarianism with empty gestures of grass roots populism.)

But there is something else of particular note that each of these divergent cultures actually share in that is symptomatic — not of their apparent oppositional natures — but rather of their rhythm, their unrecognized harmony. I do not think that this mutual participation is necessarily symmetrical or even obvious. But, and nevertheless, it is the very existence and continued reproduction of the contemporary heroin crisis — a *bona fide* national crisis that has ravaged countless American lives and communities since the dawn of the 21st century — that can serve as the frame by which we can better perceive both this emergent cultural divide and their mutual immersion in what can only be characterized as the absolute reality of globalized Capital in the 21st century:

> **From the way the Santa Cruz cops talk about it, the security camera video that captured a reputed high-price call girl injecting the 51-year-old tech veteran with a fatal dose of the drug aboard his yacht in Santa Cruz was surely horrific. But it was particularly chilling for another reason:**
>
> **While the seven-minute-long death scene drew a final curtain on the life of the father of five, it raised another on a dark and largely hidden side of Silicon Valley in 2014. With a booming startup culture cranked up by fiercely competitive VPs and adrenaline-driven coders, and a tendency for stressed-out managers to look the other way, illicit drugs and black-market painkillers have become part of the landscape here in the world's frothy fountain of tech.[4]**

What is most shocking about the above passage — other than the proximity of the human tragedy revealed by the event's details — is that such a story runs directly contra to the standard narrative of the American opiate crisis: that it is a crisis of the white working class; that it is a crisis to be found in depressed mining communities and former factory towns; or, that it is a crisis that symbolically chronicles the socioeconomic and cultural decline of the American middle class in an emergent global society. That is to say, heroin is by no means seen as being representative of successful tech entrepreneurs and expensive yachts off the California coast, but rather that of broken-down and hopeless working class American communities that are now suffering the consequences of a dual crime in a rapidly globalizing world: having no viable way to directly access the global economy and being ideologically out of step with the multiculturalism, social fluidity, and borderless nature of neoliberal globalization:

> **Here's the frightening thing about Pennsylvania's heroin epidemic: It has spread to almost every corner of the state and does not discriminate based on age.**
>
> **And it's getting worse.**
>
> **Fueled by a boom in prescription pain medicine, heroin and related drug overdoses increased by 20 percent in 2014. And based on preliminary reports to the Pennsylvania Coroner's Association, the number of overdose deaths in Pennsylvania likely increased again in 2016.**
>
> **And it isn't just in Pennsylvania. Across the nation, according to the Center for Disease Control and Prevention, opioid overdoses have quadrupled since 2000. Particularly hard hit have been Rust-Belt states and Appalachia where the number of deaths per 100,000 population are among the highest in the nation ...[5]**

This is not an argument to claim that opiate use is statistically "equal" in small town Ohio and Silicon Valley, or that heroin addiction is similarly represented in both Wall Street and Appalachia. The pointing out of two symptomatic instances of the American opiate crisis — from two drastically different demographic bases that are seen to be both diametrically and naturally opposed to one another in contemporary American society — is rather to highlight the fact that the heroin crisis is fundamentally a universal crisis; that it is perhaps *the* emblematic pathology of 21st century globalized capitalism that now lives between the crevices in the background of American life.

Information Overload

What has emerged for individuals across the spectrum in present day America is simply the mass exhaustion of their neurological capacities. Amidst today's cultural fluidity and socioeconomic dynamism, the human nervous system is simply unable to function: it is unable to keep pace with the exponential technological change and the day to day operation of contemporary global markets in their virtualized form. The sheer speed of integrated computational technologies, the hyper-competition that has been naturalized by the supply side economics central to neoliberalism, and the radical individualization of culture and community — all for the purpose of more efficient and optimized productivity within the space of global capitalist dynamics — have all done their part in radically destabilizing the contemporary American psyche.[6]

But who can realistically do this? That is to say, who can realistically keep pace with the velocity of digital time, computational logic, and global markets? And, furthermore, what happens to one's sense of self when he or she realizes that they are fundamentally not up to the task of the constant self-optimization and the generation of the unlimited productivity that neoliberalism demands of its subjects?

What happens, amongst other things, in a society that abides by such ideological and material forces is that depression and social anxiety become so prevalent that we are made to characterize these psychological pathologies as *neutral*, as naturalized features of our collective psychic terrain.[7] What this means is that the underlying causal network for the dramatic appearance of these various psychic pathologies in contemporary American society over the past several decades must necessarily be displaced from any social or economic source and reduced to a purely neurological or genetic code if one is to avoid directly encountering their systemic nature:

This pathologization already forecloses any possibility of politicization. By privatizing these problems – treating them as if they were caused only by chemical imbalances in the individual's neurology and/ or by their family background – any question of social systemic causation is ruled out.[8]

When taking such a background into account — the background of a truly epic psychological and spiritual crisis metastasizing throughout society — regarding the present-day heroin crisis, what is perhaps most interesting is the paradoxical fact that opiate addiction has actually emerged as a strategy to ward off, to cope with, and ultimately to block out these very same psychic afflictions that neoliberalism has brought forth over the past several decades. The contemporary addict uses heroin as a means to "get high," to "feel good," precisely so they won't have to experience that same sense of spiritual atomization and economic hopelessness that is now being distributed throughout American society as a fact of life. From this perspective, the contemporary heroin addict should not be perceived as just some tragic side effect of the present day socioeconomic order. More appropriately, the contemporary opiate addict should be seen as a signature product of neoliberal globalization: as a living and breathing symbol of the world we now reside in.

There is an explosion of theories — the various contemporary psychological and neurological theories that seek to frame the dramatic rise of heroin use in a purely scientific discourse — that attempt to explain to an increasingly frustrated society why such an epidemic has suddenly infected the youth of America. Unresolved psychic traumas that remain lodged in the individual's unconscious, apropos a classic Freudian reading of the situation; a genetic disposition to addiction[9] that materializes in a particular neurological composition that thus affects the opiate receptors in the brain; a result of biographical trauma that pushes the individual into a state of PTSD are a few such examples.

But what this community of experts commenting on this crisis has not sufficiently realized is the fact that so much of contemporary heroin addiction is a purely socioeconomic pathology; that it has been reproduced throughout American culture at such an astonishing pace for the exceedingly simple reason that the potential addict now views themselves as simply unable or unworthy to effectively participate in *life itself.* The young (potential) addict looks at their prospects to live a stable life, a life of basic dignity as a working or middle class American and realizes it has become the equivalent of a fool's errand.

In 1952, 1891, or even 1933 in the very heart of the Great Depression, a young American looking toward the future saw something that was at least minimally stable, perceived something that brought forth at least a minimal sense of hope for a viable economic future and the prospects for family and community life. The industrialized economy — with its large, organized spaces of Fordist production methods, with its collective bargaining that allowed for generous pensions and insurance plans, while bringing forth the reality of a common laboring class with mutual interests[10] — even for all of its faults, it nevertheless brought forth a general feeling of stability and the sense that a viable future could be perceived and experienced for the American worker.

With the transformation of capitalism from its industrial to its postindustrial phase that has been progressively developing since the 1970s, one of the principal features of this transformation has been this slow and painful cancellation of the future;[11] this foreclosure of an imagined future for both individuals and society at large.

And now, immersed in the reality of 21st century America under the ideological force of neoliberal globalization, this looming sense of permanent instability has become the lived experience for nearly all Americans. The reduction of long term employment into an ever increasing precarious and contractual labor market,[12] the ideological reconstitution of the

American worker into "an entrepreneur of the self," and the incredible indeterminacy and disruption central to global technology has forced human consciousness into what can only be described as a temporal box — this strange life that we now collectively live where even the most horrifying stories only last in our awareness for a 24 hour news cycle, a society that tries to manage itself living paycheck to paycheck — have all done their part in completely undermining our ability to even imagine an intentional life in the era of globalized capitalism.

What we are speaking of here is a transformation that is so fundamental to the reality of our day to day experience that we have suddenly found ourselves quite literally "thrown into" a whole new world, a new horizon of meaning that we have not yet fully grasped:

Today's society is no longer Foucault's disciplinary world of hospitals, madhouses, prisons, barracks, and factories. It has long been replaced by another regime, namely a society of fitness studios, office towers, banks, airports, shopping malls, and genetic laboratories. Twenty-first-century society is no longer a disciplinary society, but rather an achievement society. And its inhabitants are no longer "obedience-subjects" but "achievement-subjects." They are entrepreneurs of themselves ...

Disciplinary society is still governed by no. Its negativity produces madmen and criminals. In contrast, achievement society creates depressives and losers.[13]

But such a society not only creates "depressives" and "losers," it also creates addicts, *and heroin addicts specifically*. But in gravitating to heroin addiction — perhaps the most ruthless and unforgiving lived experience imaginable — as a strategy to ward off the very same impossible demands continually leveled by neoliberalism, the addict only lives out an exaggerated and more directly brutal version of the very thing he has so adamantly refused to participate in: the daily "achievement" of somehow getting the next fix.

In 21st century America, heroin addiction has become perhaps the signature socialized pathology, like a fact of life that has come to define the times. And although other opiate based addictions have certainly been present in times past throughout America's history — such as the generation of Civil War soldiers returning home from the battlefield, or as represented in the literature of William Burroughs in postwar America — it is only in the emergence of neoliberal globalization where heroin addiction will rise to the level of what could even be considered as normalized.

And, just as addiction has become the signature social pathology, so has the heroin addict become one of the emblematic subjectivities of the times. Surrounded by the innumerable floating signifiers and semiotic vacancies that define our global consumer society, the contemporary heroin addict is like a person moving through a rummage heap in search of some semblance of meaning,[14] and only tragically able to find it artificially in the act of getting high.

The purpose of what follows is thus to trace a line of this very development: to meditate and reflect upon both the material and ideological forces that now compose contemporary American society and then relate why such forces would be so very conducive to the emergence and sustainment of a heroin epidemic throughout its culture.

Tony Robbins as the Prophet of Neoliberalism

The reaction to a life that has become bare and radically fleeting occurs

as hyperactivity, hysterical work, and production. The acceleration of

contemporary life also plays a role in the lack of being. The society

of laboring and achievement is not a free society. It generates new

constraints. Ultimately, the dialectic of master and slave does not yield

a society where everyone is free and capable of leisure, too. Rather,

it leads to a society in which the master himself has become a laboring

slave. In this society of compulsion, everyone carries a work camp

inside. This labor camp is defined by the fact that it is simultaneously

prisoner and guard, victim and perpetrator. One exploits oneself.[15]

— Byung Chul Han

Sometimes it seems as if an alien voice has infected humanity over the past thirty years. It is a merciless, ruthless voice that demands of its subjects constant self-optimization, endless personal innovation, and boundless productivity;[16] all the while transforming nearly all public space into a topography of pure competition in which humanity is subjected to a theory that rests upon the notion that human life is equal to the law of the jungle: a dog eat dog world where only the strong survive. Although a certain kind of competition has always been inherent to the development of capitalism (and one should also mention here the fact that in contrast to a purely capitalist mode of competition there is absolutely a life affirming kind of competition as well, such as in the competition central to athletics) what we are referring to here is a completely new iteration and intensification of the competition principal in which *life itself*,[17] not strictly the domain of economic production, has become subject to this competitive law.

Although this has always been the core fantasy of capitalism — to create a world of pure, unregulated competition between various economic interests — in times past the technology simply wasn't advanced enough to make this fantasy actualized. For example, in the era of the factory, the productive symbol throughout the period of the industrialized economy, the energy of capitalism had difficulty extending itself past the 9-5 shift or beyond the perimeter of the factory and into the personal lives of its workers. In this period, capitalism was equally constrained by both the physical boundary of the factory (or the office building) and the regimentation of time that was utilized to measure the labor that was performed within that very same space of production. But today, with the advent of networked technologies and the various corporate platforms[18] that have come to define the global economy in the second decade of the 21st century — networks and platforms that are constantly circulating information and flows of capital throughout every nook and cranny of social space — the temporal and spatial boundaries that once constrained capitalism have been effectively obliterated.

It is within this novel dynamic, a dynamic in which the core drive of capitalism has become synchronized with a newfound technical capacity, that has opened up the possibility in which

… "competition" became the crucial word for the economy, whose project was to submit human relationships to the singular imperative of competition. The term itself became naturalized to the point where saying "competition" was like saying "work." But competition is not the same as work. Competition is like crime, like violence, like murder, like rape. Competition equals war. Gilles Deleuze and Félix Guattari say that fascism is "when a war machine is installed in each hole, in every niche." And I would say that an economic regime based on competition is fascism perfected. But how does this violence arrive in the economic sphere?[19]

In this rapid turn towards a humanity mediated by *pure competition*, one can only marvel at the lengths that the ruling ideological order will go to normalize this pathological reconstitution of civil society; making unregulated competition seem like a natural fact of life that should be admired as a prototype for success in business, relationships, and all of our personal endeavors. Not only are we to accept this transformation, we are to embody it and actualize it in every waking moment. Case in point is the following passage from *New York Times* columnist Thomas Friedman and his investigations into the new business practices of the contemporary global economy:

> **I had that experience in 2014 when I decided to write a column about General Electric's research center in Niskayuna, New York. Every engineering team looks like one of those multiethnic Benetton ads. But this was not affirmative action at work; it was a brutal meritocracy. But when you are competing in the global technology Olympics every day, you have to recruit the best talent from anywhere you can find it.[20]**

Even Friedman can't help, in a classic instance of a Freudian slip, to refer to a system he is unabashedly praising as being "brutal." And it *is* brutal, as further articulated in the following passage by Wendell Berry, the great American writer and farmer, perhaps the ultimate voice of decency and humility in present day American society:

> **The question that we finally come to is a practical one, though it is not one that is entirely answerable by empirical methods: Can a university, or a nation, afford this exclusive rule of**

competition, this purely economic economy? The great fault of this approach to things is that it is so drastically reductive; it does not permit us to live and work as human beings, as the best of our inheritance defines us. Rats and roaches live by competition under the law of supply and demand; it is the privilege of human beings to live under the laws of justice and mercy. It is impossible not to notice how little the proponents of the ideal of competition have to say about honesty, which is the fundamental economic virtue, and how very little they have to say about community, compassion, and mutual help.[21]

It is important to reiterate that the all-encompassing deregulation and subsequent radicalization of the competition principal that has been absolutely paramount to the ongoing project of neoliberalism from the beginning is *not* just what pertains to the basic functioning of the global economy — as in the deregulation that has allowed countless factories throughout America's Rust Belt to migrate to the de-unionized labor markets of Asia and Latin America — it is also what pertains to our private lives and our very interior experiences as human beings: in neoliberalism, *we compete to live and live to compete.* And because of that very shift in our collective perception of how life "should be" — in the way we are now ideologically interpellated by social authority to regard our lives and the society that we live in — basic morality, basic decency, and basic civility is now being foreclosed across all of our social and cultural spaces in favor of this violent, competitive law.[22]

What a writer like Thomas Friedman ultimately bears witness to — both in the above passage and throughout the body of his writing — is simply the pervasiveness, and therefore invisibility, of this very same "voice." All of the "brutality" that now undergirds the "global meritocracy" — along with all of the psychic, social, and ecological devastation it produces — is casually passed over in favor of a never ending praise of the radically heightened productivity, the exponentially increased efficiency of market operations, and the multiple advances in labor saving innovation and therefore corporate profitability. Never once does Friedman question in any serious way the underlying axioms of this new ideological constellation. He simply performs his duty as a loyal soldier, an ideologue *par excellence* of neoliberal globalization by attempting to make it palatable and appearing as "normal" for his vast readership. But it is *not* normal. And this is exactly what must be said today loudly and unapologetically. Friedman's individual voice simply gives particular content to the universality of the neoliberal voice itself, and the popularity of his writing speaks in no uncertain terms to how this voice has become the officially sanctioned soundtrack to our lives within the era of 21st century globalized capitalism.

But when trying to account for the incredibly damaging emotional and psychic effect this "voice" has had upon your life, relationships, and economic stability, whatever you do *don't* listen to your therapist's claims that this is just the relentless voice of the unsatisfied Freudian ego, the primary psychological model present throughout the industrial era of human productivity, an era that was fundamentally structured upon the notion of repression rather than the notion of constant achievement and unregulated competition that has come to define the present.

The psychic triad of the Id—Ego—Superego as Freud schematized it, was not just the signature model of the human mind throughout the period of industrialized capitalism, it also bore witness to the disciplinary structures that defined the economy of that time.[23] Take the workings of the factory as exemplary: the Id signified all of the various autonomous mechanical processes that composed the underlying operation of the factory space, the "unconscious" of the factory. The Ego is the worker, the conscious agent who filters, forms, and structures these mechanical processes into a valuable final product that can be brought to the market in order to maximize any and all surplus value. And the foreman is akin to the Superego, the repressive moral agent that ensures the work is being performed up to standards and that all the rules and regulations of the factory floor are being observed. Freud's psychic economy, like the factory itself, is a classic disciplinary structure that confines, represses, and molds its raw material into obedient subjects.

What we are dealing with now in the era of neoliberal globalization is something entirely different.[24] The Freudian model of repression has thus given way to a model of never ending achievement and positivity — and with that shift personal neurosis and repression has shifted towards a socialized depression and a profound cultural alienation.[25]

The society that we now find ourselves immersed in under the weight of globalized capitalism is ideologically predicated upon the *rejection* of all the old modes of repression and prohibition. It rather encourages its subjects, like the famous Apple commercial,[26] "to be different," "to be a rebel," "to change the world." But not so rebellious as to actually question these very same axiomatic rules and regulations that are now equally proclaimed by multinational corporations and life coaches alike, but to be a rebel so that you can more effectively compete within the very framework of neoliberal globalization itself.

What this "voice" really is is simply the ideological vibration that legitimizes neoliberal globalization, it is the reverberating echo of people like Tony Robbins, Bill Gates and Sheryl Sandberg: the hymn of Silicon Valley, the sound brought forth by the marketing plans of Madison Avenue, or the sound of a click when you press "Like" on your smartphone. It is these contemporary cultural and economic forces that have synchronized into a whole new "voice," *a new ideological horizon*, that we have tragically mistaken for our own.

In the 1997 film *The Usual Suspects,* Kevin Spacey's character makes the remark, "The greatest trick the Devil ever pulled was convincing the world he didn't exist." Is this not similar to the situation we find ourselves in today when contending with the neoliberal voice, that the greatest trick it ever played was getting the people of the globalized world to believe that this voice was their own; that they were they architects of its very form in addition to supplying the endless content that sustains it?

The ever-increasing fragmentation of our interior lives that has emerged as a result of the unregulated power of computational technologies becoming linked with the imperatives of globalized capitalism — and of all the precarity, disruption, and unsustainability that comes along with such an inherently violent combination — is fundamentally a problem of *structure*.[27] That is to say, it is an *objective* problem that is then routinely misdiagnosed as a *subjective* problem, a problem of our personal psychic or spiritual territory. In other words, the explosion of psychic ailments such as depression, social anxiety and bipolar disorder that have spread throughout contemporary American society like a wildfire have far less to do with our unresolved psychic traumas and particular neural compositions than we may have thought: what healthy person *wouldn't* feel a sense of anxiety or depression living in a world such as ours?

The Prophet Of Neoliberalism

If there is a singular personality that can be regarded as the true prophet of neoliberalism — the individual who has best proselytized and disseminated its basic axioms to the masses for their passive acceptance and practical adoption — it is undoubtedly Tony Robbins, the California born motivational speaker, author, and corporate trainer. But what is perhaps most interesting about Tony Robbins is the fact that one of his principal cultural effects is how he has brought forth endless new Tony Robbins's. But this cultural effect lies not only in the countless personal development coaches and motivational speakers he has spawned as a result of the multi-decade period he has spent circulating his tapes, books, and seminars throughout American and global culture as a whole, but also how we ourselves have interiorized so many of his ideas and unknowingly made them our own.

Perhaps the principal reason why someone like Tony Robbins and the entire personal development industrial-complex is so dangerous is because everything they advise, from a certain perspective, is actually true:

Reach your potential? Of course.

Become your best self? Absolutely.

Live your dreams? We should all do that.

But when you say and advise these things within the global system that we are now living within, when you say and advise these things within the framework of a hyper-competitive global capitalist dynamic, they effectively cease to be spiritual maxims on how to live a true life and start to function in a borderline sociopathic way; they start to function as a means to maximize one's instrumental value and nothing more. And this is profoundly dangerous to civil society, public life, and our collective psychological health.

In other words, why this industry, in which someone like Tony Robbins is in many ways the ultimate symbol, is so profoundly dangerous, is because *they have no knowledge that they themselves are in danger*; they have no self-knowledge that they are advocating for a system that will eventually exploit and alienate themselves as well.

So, the central problem with identifying Tony Robbins as one of the key figures who has ideologically justified the neoliberal turn is that the problem no longer resides with just Tony Robbins anymore. Almost like the character played by Michael Keaton in the 1996 film *Multiplicity* who endlessly self-replicates variations of his primary self, Robbins has (even though we can be sure he takes total credit for it) unknowingly birthed an entire generation of personal coaches, speakers, and corporate gurus who all engage in a similar theme: to get their clientele to fully embrace neoliberal ideology by systematically avoiding its obvious antagonisms and symptomatic pathologies. His act, at its core, is a system of personal development that is designed to avoid the possibility of one's exploitation by the Other and rather joyfully engage in the task of *self-exploitation instead*:[28] to optimize one's neural pathways, to become more efficient in one's personal relations, to become like a productive machine that engages in a series of endless projects to fully realize one's potential:

> **I realized that we all need a word to anchor ourselves to the focus of Constant and Never-ending Improvement. When we create a word, we encode meaning and create a way of thinking. The words that we use consistently make up the fabric of how we think and even affect our decision making. As a result of this understanding, I created a simple mnemonic: CANI!™ (pronounced kuhn-EYE), which stands for Constant And Never-ending Improvement.[29]**

Robbins is here giving voice to a paradigm shift taking place at a very precise moment in time — the above is a passage taken from his 1992 book *Awaken the Giant Within* — in which the mode of capitalism that had been present during its postwar Keynesian, industrial phase was then transforming into its postindustrial, networked based phase; a change that began rapidly occurring in the 1980s and then became the unquestionable norm by the 1990s. This "constant and never-ending improvement" that Robbins speaks of could never occur in an economy defined by union labor, factories, and an organizational principal that ran itself along a bureaucratic, Fordist model. "Constant and never ending improvement" as a maxim of how to organize one's life and work rather explodes into the consciousness of American business and culture at the very moment when those old industrial categories start to dissolve and the neoliberal model — a model of private entrepreneurialism, individualized consumerism, and where watchwords such as flexibility, creativity, and fluidity would be introduced as the core principals of big business — began to mobilize.[30]

Franco "Bifo" Berardi has characterized the 1990s — the very decade when Tony Robbins became a worldwide phenomenon, along with the crystallization of neoliberal capitalism as the only game in town following the collapse of communism and Eastern European socialism — as "the Prozac economy": a time of unbounded optimism based on the false premise that the neoliberal model could continue on indefinitely into the future. But this same "Prozac economy" also coincided with a sharp rise of depression and a whole host of other acute psychopathologies that now infect global society at large:

The 1990s saw an era of increasing productivity, increasing enthusiasm for production, increasing happiness of intellectual workers, who became entrepreneurs and so forth in the dot-com mania. But the 1990s was also the Prozac decade. You cannot explain what Alan Greenspan called the "irrational exuberance" in the markets without recalling the simple fact that millions of cognitive workers were consuming tons

of cocaine, amphetamines, and Prozac throughout the 1990s. Greenspan was not speaking of the economy, but the cocaine effect in the brains of millions of cognitive workers all over the world. And the dot-com crash was the sudden disappearance of this amphetamine from the brains of those workers.[31]

We will come back to explore the disjuncture between drugs like methamphetamine and cocaine as juxtaposed against heroin, but for the time being let us simply note that the 1990s — the decade preceding the Oxycontin epidemic that eventually transformed into the heroin crisis of today — was demarcated not only by a marked increase in productivity and concentration of global capitalist development, but also by a marked increase and concentration of psychological instability and mental illness.

Notice the symmetry between former chairman of the Federal Reserve Bank Alan Greenspan, in defining global markets as behaving with "irrational exuberance" and the central axiom of Tony Robbins, the completely delusional and unsustainable goal of "constant and never-ending improvement" *within a capitalist framework*. Is not the central pillar of Tony Robbins' philosophy (CANI), which in many ways *is* the neoliberal ideal, the very definition of "irrational exuberance": a total pipe dream that was as equally delusional as the 1990s markets that saw infinite growth and expansion extending into infinity?

What we are now approaching is how this peculiar combination — of a pervasive personal development philosophy brought forth by the likes of Tony Robbins combined with the increasing power and velocity of market forces linked with networked technologies — has come to produce a very specific mode of subjectivity in contemporary Western economies, what the German-Korean philosopher Byung-Chul Han has termed "the achievement subject":

> **The achievement subject stands free from any external instance of domination forcing it to work, much less exploiting it. It is lord and master of itself. Thus, it is a subject to no one – or, as the case may be, only to itself. It differs from the obedience-subject on this score. However, the disappearance of domination does not entail freedom. Instead, *it makes freedom and constraint coincide.* Thus, the achievement-subject gives itself over to *compulsive freedom* – that is, to the *free constraint* of maximizing achievement. Excess work and performance escalate into auto-exploitation. This is more efficient than allo-exploitation, for the freedom attends it. The exploiter is simultaneously exploited. Perpetrator and victim can no longer be distinguished. Such self-referentiality produces a paradoxical freedom that abruptly switches over into violence because of the compulsive structures dwelling within it. The psychic indispositions of achievement society are pathological manifestations of such a paradoxical freedom.[32]**

The "achievement subject" appears as a social agent at the moment when the dynamics of technological change and globalized capitalism began to move at such a speed — "business at the speed of light," according to Bill Gates — that an insatiable demand for constant learning, constant training, and constant attention in an attempt to stay competitive with the rapidly developing pace of global markets and global technology becomes a necessity to effectively even survive:

> **Thriving in today's workplace is all about what LinkedIn's co-founder Reid Hoffman calls investing in "the start-up of you." No politician in America will tell you this, but every boss will: You can't just show up. You need a plan to succeed.**[33]

And this is exactly why someone like Tony Robbins, and his ever-multiplying army of motivational coaches, have become *absolutely essential* to the neoliberal order: the average person needs "motivation" to even remotely engage in such an impossible and unsustainable dynamic. More accurately: a person needs to be thoroughly deluded to believe such a task is remotely sympathetic to their mental health, economic well-being, and ability to effectively participate in civil society. We can look again to none other than Thomas Friedman to happily demonstrate the true pathological character of this system absent any self-consciousness whatsoever:

> **When I walk into a subway and see someone playing Candy Crush on their phone, I think there's a wasted five minutes when they could be bettering themselves.**[34]

In other words, don't relax, don't even take five minutes to daydream or play some silly internet game on your phone. Instead, your entire life should be entirely devoted to narcissistic improvement and economic utilitarianism so you can better function in the most socially unjust and emotionally devastating economic system in the history of the world — *this* is the ideological core of Robbins' "CANI" when stripped away to its zero point. We don't even see the insanity of it all anymore because we have become so accustomed to it.

And what is lost in this scenario in our never-ending quest to assert our individuality through constant achievement, to feel the constant need to prove our self-worth within the channels of our various professional and social networks? What is lost, what is absolutely devastated, is none other than the very heart of our self-worth and basic psychic identity:

Identity today is not what it was even twenty years ago. It pops up as autofill suggestions in drop-down menus. It is intensified by punitive quantification, by viral lynch mobs, material deprivation, browser memory. Traditional identities ran on race, class, gender, plain loyalty, money, or memory. Contemporary ones add proprietary operating systems to this mix. How is your newsfeed organized? Your loyalty scheme? How does your credit score soar or shrink? Who owns your interactions or opinions? To know yourself and kin today, forget about a shaman or a shrink. You might need a Ukrainian hacker.[35]

The symbolic and psychological chaos that is now acutely felt across all layers of the social body is a *bona fide* crisis in the making. The increasing reach of technology and capitalism into our brains and bodies, the reduction of culture and politics into soundbites and Twitter feeds, the transformation of human love and human relationships into technical instruments of market efficiency (the left/right swipe of Tinder is representative of this shift) — such changes are creating an almost unspeakable sense of both irrelevance and impotence for the contemporary human psyche. The only way out of this impossible predicament, in the experience of the majority of cognitive professionals across Western economies, is to double down and engage in an endless series of projects, self-improvement courses, and different methodologies so to further optimize one's self-production.

This is the ideological horizon within which the contemporary heroin addict finds himself. She finds herself in a world where everyone now seems to want to *become their best self, to live to their full potential, to discover their power within* — **within a capitalist horizon.** What these sentiments bear witness to is not simply the underlying purpose of ancient spiritualities in contemporary terms, but rather to disclose the basic operation of Capital in the 21st century. As global technology and global capitalism become further enmeshed in all networks of exchange, what emerges is an abstract power that exponentially individualizes people, ideologically transforms them into instruments of the market —— as an assemblage of neurons versus a living human being — and reconstitutes their subjectivity as a quantifiable entity that can be coded and exchanged. Such objective and material violence utterly destroys the stability of the Ego and thus calls for either pseudo-spiritual remedies or pharmacological interventions to mitigate the socialized suffering.

And, perhaps most importantly, it has created a scenario where the voice of pure competition now reigns supreme: the contemporary heroin addict emerges in direct response to these socioeconomic and ideological forces.

Heroin Addiction And Capitalism

The opiate addict exploded into the cultural matrix of American society in the first decade of the 21st century as a subject who spoke to the rejection of neoliberalism and its incessant demands. In this sense, the contemporary heroin addict is not purely a psychological casualty — a victim of some earlier biographical trauma or a person with some kind of innate neurological dysfunction that then seeks refuge in addiction — the addict is also fundamentally a political casualty. Although the crisis of heroin addiction is undoubtedly a sign that bears witness to the slow and steady decomposition of the social brain — our collective mental vitality, the "general intellect" as Marx would say — what it really speaks to is the *crisis of capitalism itself.* The heroin addict emerges as a highly visible social-symbolic agent, not only at the moment when capitalism seems to be collapsing, but at the moment when it also becomes the unquestioned reality and all-encompassing mediator of our lives:

Capitalism is what is left when beliefs have collapsed at the level of ritual or symbolic elaboration, and all that is left is the consumer-spectator, trudging through the ruins and relics.[36]

The accelerating compulsion to circulate capital and have formal techno-logical mediation through every nook and cranny of our lives has resulted in, to use again the terminology of Thomas Friedman, a "flattened world": a world that is pathologically fixated on smoothing out all jagged edges and inconsistencies in order to fully optimize market dynamism while fully operating within the coordinates of the global technology apparatus. But amidst this universal "flatness" a whole range of the most violent psy-chopathologies are now exploding across the cultural surface and indicat-ing that all is not well behind the shiny curtain of 21st century globalized capitalism.

It is interesting to notice the near perfect symmetrical relationship between the core drives of both heroin addiction and capitalism. The addictive potential of heroin lies in the drug's ability to effectively mimic, and then greatly exaggerate, the naturally occurring endorphins in the human nervous system. Endorphins are a class of chemical compounds found throughout the CNS (Central Nervous System) whose primary function is to regulate the experience of pleasure and pain. Certain neu-rons in the brain have receptors that match certain endorphins, almost like two pieces of a puzzle, that are able to latch on to each other and pro-duce a specific chemical reaction that then relays a message to the body: "this experience feels good," "this experience is painful."[37]

What heroin does when it enters into the organism is to essentially impersonate the body's naturally occurring endorphins, which then makes it able to bind to the neural receptors in the brain that are associ-ated with the experience of pleasure. The problem for the body, and why heroin precipitates such an intense feeling of euphoria, is that the brain is unable to effectively regulate this sudden flood of endorphin-like compounds: the experience of pleasure is put into an artificially induced state of overdrive.[38]

But the real problem lies in the fact that once heroin is continually injected (or sniffed, smoked, etc.) into the body for a period of time, once a pattern of consistent use is established, the body begins to stop producing its own endorphins. The body effectively mis-recognizes the foreign agency of heroin as its own biologically produced endorphins and thus starts to reduce its own production. And not only that, but because each injection of heroin is essentially a surge of new endorphins, the body starts to *produce new opiate receptors as well.*[39]

This is, for all intents and purposes, the vicious cycle of addiction in a nutshell. The viciousness lies in the fact that you are always in need of a higher *quantity* of chemical agents to produce the same *quality* of feeling: as the number of neural receptors increase, so too does the need for endorphins to bind to them and thus bring forth the desired feeling.

In a slight shift of perspective, this is almost the exact same operation of capitalism at its elementary level, in that you are always in need of more sites of capital investment to produce the same level of profit. That is to say, what addiction and Capital both share in is *the production of a desire that is structurally insatiable*, a desire that is structurally impossible to ever fill in a sustainable way, which then produces a series of externalized antagonisms: stealing from your mother's pocketbook, outsourcing a productive factory to a Third World sweatshop.

For the active heroin addict, caught in the grip of a debilitating spiritual pathology in which all logic and sense is progressively stripped away, the only thing that can solve the personal crisis of active addiction is *more* heroin. In the precise same way, for contemporary global capitalism, caught in the grips of its own self-produced crisis in which all logic and sense is being progressively stripped away from the entirety of humanity, the only thing that can alleviate the social dislocation and economic inequality innate to globalized capitalism is *more* globalized capitalism: more loans from the IMF, more capital investment from Goldman Sachs into emergent markets, more of our personal lives mediated by platforms such as Uber, Facebook, and Airbnb.

Notice the homology present: the active addict is submerged in a dynamic by which the condition of its impossibility — the absolute impossibility of ever living a happy and stable life as an active addict— is only produced by the condition of its possibility: the fact that the only time the illusion of living a potentially happy and fulfilling life as an active addict is possible is in the immediate moments after the high of the shot first takes hold, the very moment when the addict is thinking most irrationally. It is the dialectical tension between the possible and the impossible that motors the essence of addiction.[40]

And with globalized capitalism the same logic applies: the condition of its impossibility — the impossibility of a local community, nation state, or global society ever functioning as a healthy and sustainable culture when subsumed under the power of Capital — is only brought forth by its condition of possibility, on the happy day when the stock market rises on news of a monthly jobs uptick and people are deluded enough to believe that the system is actually working.[41]

This is the spiraling dynamic that the contemporary heroin addict has found themselves in.

But it is also the dynamic that they have found themselves desperately wanting to escape from.

GETTING HIGH IN THE CONTROL SOCIETY

> *The problem is no longer getting people to express themselves, but*
> *providing little gaps of solitude and silence in which they might*
> *eventually find something to say. Repressive forces don't stop people*
> *from expressing themselves, but rather, force them to express*
> *themselves. What a relief to have nothing to say, the right to say*
> *nothing, because only then is there a chance of framing the rare, or*
> *ever rarer, the thing that might be worth saying.*[42]
>
> — *Gilles Deleuze*

Gilles Deleuze's 1990 essay "Postscript on the Societies of Control" centers on the transition between the "disciplinary societies" described by Michel Foucault — the socioeconomic model present throughout the period of industrialized capitalism — and what Deleuze characterized as "societies of control": the now operative structure of contemporary Western society defined by the presence of digital technologies and networked capitalism.

Disciplinary societies emerged within the greater frame of industrialized capitalism and were demarcated by a series of "spaces of enclosure": such as the factory, the government bureaucracy, the military barracks, the boxing gym,[43] the nuclear family, etc. Each of these enclosed systems had its own system of rules and regulations and its own particular spatial boundaries, to which the individual would continually pass while moving from one to another. Disciplinary societies reach their high point in the mid 20th century before starting to slowly breakdown following the Second World War. And by 1990, just as Deleuze was writing his now famous essay, these spaces and institutions that had been previously constituted by a disciplinary logic were in their final days; in process of being replaced by the logic and discourses of an emergent control society — networked technologies, postindustrial capitalism, multinational corporations, the social medias, etc.

Deleuze speaks about the difference between disciplinary logic and the logic of control in the following passage:

The factory [symbolic of disciplinary societies] constituted individuals as a single body to the double advantage of the boss who surveyed each element within the mass and the unions who mobilized a mass resistance; but the corporation [symbolic of control societies] constantly presents the

brashest rivalry as a healthy form of emulation, an excellent motivational force that opposes individuals against one another and runs through each, dividing each within … Indeed, just as the corporation replaces the factory, perpetual training tends to replace the school, and continuous control to replace the examination, which is the surest way of delivering the school over to the corporation.

In the disciplinary societies one was always starting again (from school to the barracks, from the barracks to the factory), while in the societies of control one is never finished with anything—the corporation, the educational system, the armed services being metastable states coexisting in one and the same modulation, like a universal system of deformation.[44]

The mode in which social authority once regulated the interrelation between the various enclosures and processes that constituted industrialized capitalism —- the "solid" form of capitalism (factories, bureaucracies, 9-5 shifts, etc.) as compared to contemporary globalized capitalism that functions in a more "gaseous" or "liquid"[45] manner (networks, data, personal entrepreneurialism, working from your smartphone at a cafe, etc.) — was that of *discipline.* According to Michel Foucault discipline is the methodology by which power reproduced itself throughout the period of industrialized capitalism. All the institutions that once predominated during this period of time — the military, the school, the office bureaucracy, the factory, the prison, etc. — were enclosed spaces that *disciplined* the people placed under their command. Discipline was a process of normalization, conformity, and obedience:

All major disciplinary machinery – barracks, schools, workshops and prisons – are machines that permit the identification of the individual, know who he is, what he does, what we can do, where to place him, how to place him among the others.[46]

In other words, the disciplinary *praxis* central to the industrial economies of the 19th and much of the 20th century (up until the 1980s) was not only that which was specifically geared to address the prevalent socioeconomic relations — to regulate the manner of how one would behave in the parish church, the government office, the factory floor, the boxing gym, etc. — it was also what actively produced a particular subjectivity that mirrored that very same disciplinary logic: the society of discipline not only brought forth, for example, the boxing gym as one of its primary symbolic institutional enclosures, but also the very consciousness of the boxer as well.[47]

However, with the rise of neoliberalism in recent decades — the rise of an all-encompassing globalized capitalism mediated by the streams of images, data, and corporate advertisements that define our social media feeds and their underlying computational processes — the use of disciplinary logic to regulate society and produce a corresponding consciousness is no longer possible, or even necessary to the operation of capitalism in the present. Such a logic like discipline can no longer effectively function as it did throughout the period of the industrialized economy. The near total collapse of the emblematic disciplinary institutions that once defined Western economies — the nuclear family is replaced for single Tinder swiper; the neighborhood parish church for the chain yoga studio; the factory for the internet start-up — and the corresponding rise of a near total socioeconomic "deregulation" has brought forth a need for a new methodology of power to exert itself across the social body. This new method is what Gilles Deleuze has identified as *control*.

So where *discipline* governed the era of industrialized capitalism, today, it is *control* that mediates our present day situation; where discipline regulated our bodies, control regulates our minds, hearts, and very souls.

Deleuze further differentiates the two systems in the following lengthy passage:

Nineteenth-century capitalism is a capitalism of concentration, for production and for property. It therefore erects the factory as a space of enclosure, the capitalist being the owner of the means of production but also, progressively, the owner of other spaces conceived through analogy (the worker's familial house, the school).

As for markets, they are conquered sometimes by specialization, sometimes by colonization, sometimes by lowering the costs of production. But, in the present situation, capitalism is no longer involved in production, which it often

relegates to the Third World, even for the complex forms of textiles, metallurgy, or oil production. It's a capitalism of higher-order production. It no longer buys raw materials and no longer sells the finished products: it buys the finished products or assembles parts. What it wants to sell is services and what it wants to buy is stocks. This is no longer a capitalism for production but for the product, which is to say, for being sold or marketed. Thus it is essentially dispersive, and the factory has given way to the corporation. The family, the school, the army, the factory are no longer the distinct analogical spaces that converge towards an owner—state or private power—but are coded figures—deformable and transformable—of a single corporation that now has only stockholders ...

Marketing has become the center or the "soul" of the corporation. We are taught that corporations have a soul, which is the most terrifying news in the world. The operation of markets is now the instrument of social control and forms the impudent breed of our masters. Control is short-term and of rapid rates of turnover, but also continuous and without limit, while discipline was of long duration, infinite and discontinuous. Man is no longer man enclosed, but man in debt. It is true that capitalism has retained as a constant the extreme poverty of three-quarters of humanity, too poor

for debt, too numerous for confinement: control will not only have to deal with erosions of frontiers but with the explosions within shanty towns or ghettos.[48]

This transformation of social relations and ideological conditioning (a conditioning that Deleuze clearly saw rapidly developing in the early 1990s when he penned the above passage) is human life itself recast as a permanent modulation, as a never ending "project" that continually morphs and shifts in response to the movements of markets and the interventions of technology into the lives of human beings.[49] Amidst such an inherently unstable situation how does social and political authority now regulate its own substance? That is to say: how is contemporary culture made to conform to power and ideology if the methods of discipline are no longer possible in our neoliberal world?

The answer as to how we are made to conform to power in control societies is actually a counter-intuitive answer: *we are constantly ideologically programmed to be non-conformers;* we are constantly encouraged to be creative in all of our affairs, to openly express our deepest selves, and to uniquely brand ourselves so we can more efficiently compete in the global marketplace.

Discipline— the regulation of space, form, and bodies through a series of interrelated institutional spaces and processes — is no longer even conceivable in the age of neoliberal globalization and control societies: how can one even think to "discipline" a liquid such as free-flowing water; how can one even think to discipline part time coders and self-employed information workers — members of the contemporary creative class — as one would have disciplined a collective of automotive workers on a Detroit assembly line one hundred years ago?

Of course one cannot.

So, to exert power in a society based on free-flowing information and unregulated global markets, the entire breadth and scope of the disciplinary apparatus that once centered around institutional spaces of enclosure has now given way to the discourses of control. In other words, today, our lives and bodies are no longer *disciplined* as they were in our industrial past. Instead, we are *controlled* through a subtle exchange of digital networks, corporate surveillance, and from the de-centered influence of the global media apparatus.

In his 2015 book *Control,* Seb Franklin elaborates on this ideological reorientation central to the dynamic of our present society:

... control is understood as a logical substrate grounding a number of discourses in which the boundary of the workplace as a site of the apprehension and exploitation of the worker's labor disperses, so that life is understood as both uniform and fully representable in digital form, and is thus subject to value extraction across expanded fields of time and space. From the point of view afforded by control, labor is not a compression or digitization of life in certain times and places (the factory, the working day). Instead, all of

life—or, at least, all that matters about life—appears already fully digital and thus intelligible as value-creating labor. Concepts such as immaterial labor, cognitive capitalism, and post-Fordist production, as well as the neoliberal vision of the world as a constantly shifting complex of markets, can thus be understood as symptoms of this basic fundamentalism of the digital.[50]

But what Franklin does *not* refer to in this passage explicitly, although he alludes to it in innumerable ways, is that by re-conceptualizing the human being as representable in "digital" form — i.e. by extending and dispersing labor beyond its confinement in time and space (beyond the confines of the factory or the office building, and beyond the temporal limits of the "9-5" work shift), and by orienting oneself to the constantly shifting dynamics of global markets versus sites of fixed capital regulated by the state as was the case in the disciplinary model — the human psyche becomes constantly under siege, it becomes *gaseous and liquefied,*[51] and thus in need of a substance or process to alleviate the looming sense of catastrophe: this is precisely where heroin emerges into 21st century culture. And it emerges less as just a drug, just a narcotic to "get high," but rather as a means to block out this same material instability and ideological interpellation.

The Desire For Negativity

What this collapse of disciplinary logic and the rise of the control model ultimately entails, in the words of the contemporary German-Korean philosopher Byung-Chul Han, is the collapse of *negativity* itself; that is to say, in practical terms, the collapse of all the prohibitory agents that were once responsible for the regulation of society. We have been led into an age — in direct correspondence with the rise of the Deleuzian concept of control societies — of *pure positivity*: an age in which not only all of the barriers and restraints to both personal self-expression and unfettered capitalist reproduction have been obliterated, but that life itself has migrated into a technological horizon. What this means is that the violence that we are now besieged with is not the violence of negativity that was once the calling card of disciplinary logic — "You must not," said the factory foreman, the stern school principal, or the authoritative Father — but rather a new kind of violence which is central to the logic of control: "Yes you can," said the liberal politician, the motivational speaker, or the social media meme.

What constitutes this shift from "You must not" to "Yes you can"[52] is that there is no longer a clearly defined Other to which we are to resist, there is no longer a clear representation of an external agent of prohibition or repression to whom we are to respond. The days of the no nonsense factory foreman, office manager, or Father imposing a series of rigidly defined protocols upon us are now over. Instead, we have been given a sudden *carte blanche* to freely post our ideas on our virtual networks, show our sleeve tattoos, and wear yoga pants in the office; we are now strangely encouraged to continually express our creativity, openly articulate the deepest desires of our inner selves, and "to be a disruptor" even while on the job. But the ruthless factory foreman has not completely disappeared since giving way to the more "mindful" and "conscious" postmodern office manager. Han's point is that we ourselves have slowly become our own "factory foreman," endlessly demanding of *ourselves* to achieve the impossible dream of a Tony Robbins lecture. This is what Han calls the *violence of positivity*:

> **The violence of positivity that derives from overproduction, overachievement, and over-communication is no longer "viral." Immunology offers no way of approaching the phenomenon. Rejection in occurring to excess positivity does not amount to immunological defense, but to digestive-neuronal abreaction and refusal. Likewise, exhaustion, fatigue, and suffocation – when too much exists – do not constitute immunological reactions. These phenomena constitute neuronal power, which is not viral because it does derive from immunological negativity …**
>
> **The violence of positivity does not presume or require hostility. It unfolds specifically in a permissive and pacified society. Consequently, it proves more invisible than immunology.[53]**

The above passage is key in terms of framing the contemporary heroin crisis in a new way. This crisis has always been thought in terms of "immunology." The heroin addict is naturally perceived as simply a sick person with an internal pathology caused by an external agent (heroin, the drug dealer, Mexican cartels, etc.) that then precipitates the inability to regulate their own psychic desires, thus being thrown into a vicious cycle of repro-duction — the basic mechanism of any addiction.

Although this definition will always be somewhat apropos to some-thing like heroin addiction, it nevertheless fails to articulate the driving social energy behind this epidemic at this particular moment in time. The heroin addict is not strictly a victim of negativity; that is to say, a victim of Otherness. The contemporary heroin addict can also be seen as a victim that symbolizes the dangers of excess positivity: the individual who ulti-mately refuses to participate in the neoliberal world of pure positivity, of pure competition, and then becomes in need of something to mitigate the overwhelming sense of exclusion from the predominant ideological order. This is exactly what Han is referring to when he says, "Rejection in occur-ring to excess positivity does not amount to immunological defense, but to digestive-neuronal abreaction and refusal."[54]

To put this concept in everyday terms: not everyone wants to spend every moment of their life trying to "become their best self" as defined by the discourses of global capitalism. But this is precisely the positivity that constitutes the functioning of control societies today. Control societ-ies are supposed to be smooth and flat, they are supposed to be "friction-less"[55] as the digital circuitry of the market is allegedly able to mediate all of our needs and interactions with the Other. But what actually happens is that the Other effectively disappears within this system and we are left with a society populated by a collection of individuals desperate to be recognized, desperate for their LinkedIn profile to stand out from the crowd.

The true violence of neoliberal globalization, of 21st century globalized capitalism, and for that matter societies of control, is that it makes everything and anything interchangeable and equalized. It makes anything and everything trackable, quantifiable, and accounted for within a system of pure exchange.

But, it accomplishes this miracle through the ultimate sleight of hand: by tricking people into thinking that by effectively "branding themselves" they can escape this system of pure exchange and become a singularity; yet, they end up becoming even more immeshed within it.

The heroin addict, from one vantage point, does escape this system. He lives off the grid. She scrapes and scrounges to eke out a life as an addict. He functions as a traumatized singularity in an emergent world of Sameness. But yet from another vantage point the addict expresses the underlying sentiment of this system in a more direct and brutal way: is not the life of a heroin addict the very neoliberal ideal, the true representation of an "everyman for himself," "deregulated" existence?

The real point is that the Sameness that now constitutes the social and economic center of 21st century capitalism in America *leads directly to the experience of the heroin addict*:

The elimination of all negativity is a hallmark of contemporary society. Everything is smoothed out. Communication, too, is smoothed out into an exchange of pleasantries; negative feelings such as sorrow are denied any language, any expression ...

> Inward orientation renders superfluous the constant comparisons with other people to which humans guided from without are compelled.[56]

Adderall as the Counter To Heroin

In order to further understand the contemporary heroin epidemic we must frame it as part of a dialectical relationship to another drug of the times that we are now living through. That is to say, we must posit it against another drug that has also risen to near epidemic proportions in contemporary society — but yet in an entirely different way and for an entirely different reason. If heroin is now the emblematic drug for the outsider — the individual who primarily exists on the periphery of globalized capitalism, unable and unwilling to fully participate in its day to day operation — then the Adderall junkie is the consummate drug of choice for the insider *par excellence*; the drug of choice for the person who not only desperately wants to participate, but the person who adamantly refuses to quit, the person who is fixated on *thriving*.[57] Day traders, students at prestigious New England prep schools, and corporate lawyers working late into the night preparing for litigation: these are just some of the contemporary subjectivities that constitute the core of Adderall addiction:

> But in interviews, dozens of people in a wide spectrum of professions said they and co-workers misused stimulants like Adderall, Vyvanse and Concerta to improve work

performance. Most spoke on the condition of anonymity for fear of losing their jobs or access to the medication.

Doctors and medical ethicists expressed concern for misusers' health, as stimulants can cause anxiety, addiction and hallucinations when taken in high doses. But they also worried about added pressure in the workplace — where the use by some pressures more to join the trend.

Elizabeth, a Long Island native in her late 20s, said that to not take Adderall while competitors did would be like playing tennis with a wood racket.

"It is necessary — necessary for survival of the best and the smartest and highest-achieving people," Elizabeth said. She spoke on the condition that she be identified only by her middle name.

Most users who were interviewed said they got pills by feigning symptoms of A.D.H.D., a disorder marked by severe impulsivity and inattention, to physicians who casually write prescriptions without proper evaluations. Others got them from friends or dealers.[58]

"It's necessary for survival," Elizabeth said. But to be more precise: it is necessary for survival *only* within a hyper-competitive capitalist framework. Adderall works on the biochemical level in a completely different way than heroin. Whereas heroin draws the user into a state of euphoria and mental detachment, Adderall radically increases concentration, cognitive processing, and psychic energy levels while decreasing the need for sleep and suppressing the user's appetite. The use of Adderall increases the activity of several neurotransmitters in the brain, such as serotonin, norepinephrine, and most especially dopamine.[59] It is a pharmacological agent that induces dramatic changes in dopamine activity in the CNS that reorganizes the brain's capacity to experience pleasure, to experience a "reward." This is the crucial difference: whereas heroin, *in itself,* is the reward, Adderall externalizes the reward into the social field, thus allowing for the radically increased productive potential while using this drug: Adderall is not the reward, *the following production is.*

Although both drugs are highly addictive and dangerous in their own way, perhaps what may constitute the true difference between heroin and Adderall is that Adderall is part and parcel of the pharmaceutical industrial complex whereas heroin is the archetypal illegal drug. Adderall is prescribed to children as young as three years old to treat symptoms of ADHD,[60] whereas even the thought of giving a child heroin would be considered monstrous and inhumane. What this signifies is that Adderall is ideologically legitimized within neoliberal space because it is so effective *in continuing to reproduce it:* the whole point of using Adderall is to become a more focused producer, to fully utilize one's latent neuronal power with laser like precision.

Heroin addiction rests on the premise of giving up, of surrendering, of passively admitting one's impotence in the face of information overload and being excluded from the capitalist order of the present. The Adderall junkie, on the other hand, is the person who absolutely refuses to quit and uses this medication specifically for that very reason. Although they too surely feel the same sense of impotence and irrelevance in response to the operation of control societies that the heroin addict does, but, instead of checking out they rather jump on the hamster wheel and engage in a never ending sprint for dear life.

Adderall addiction bears witness to the explosion of information, data, and the infinite content within the contemporary social-symbolic domain — the pathological intensification of psychic stimulation that now emanates from Madison Avenue and Silicon Valley with every new Tweet and Facebook post — that cannot be properly gauged without some kind of neural *enhancement*. In this sense, Adderall abuse cannot simply be regarded like the addiction of any other pharmacological drug, and most certainly must be regarded differently than something like heroin. It must rather be seen more like a "steroid," almost in the same way a professional athlete takes supplements to increase the presence of testosterone in their body to improve their performance. Such neural enhancements are now seen as almost a pre-requisite that is required to effectively compete in the global economy of the present:

… multitasking effect and the competitive pressure that is tied to the ability to follow the rhythm of the Infosphere are provoking the explosion of the centered self and a sort of psychotic deterritorialization of attention. The intensification of the info-flow provokes a disturbance in the cognitive ability

to detect and interpret signs, but simultaneously pushes us towards a swarm-like automation of the functioning of the mind. The self is both pressured from the outside world and replicated by the surrounding world of other minds. The faster the act of interpretation of info-stimulus, the more the process of interpretation is shared ...[61]

The dialectical axis of heroin/Adderall addiction — although in many ways they appear to be completely isolated pathologies, attracting entirely different demographics from different pharmacological compositions– should be read as being two sides of the same neoliberal coin. It is a coin in which both sides are under siege by control societies that are now thoroughly undermining the collective psychological health of contemporary American society. One side folds and descends into the nightmare of heroin addiction. The other side continues to frantically play even though their hand is bust.

American Dope

The question is frequently asked: Why does a man become a drug addict?

The answer is that he usually does not intend to become an addict. You don't wake up one morning and decide to be a drug addict. It takes at least three months' shooting twice a day to get any habit at all. And you don't really know what junk sickness is until you have had several habits. It took me almost six months to get my first habit, and then the withdrawal symptoms were mild. I think it no exaggeration to say it takes about a year and several hundred injections to make an addict.

The questions, of course, could be asked: Why did you ever try narcotics? Why did you continue using it long enough to become an addict? You become a narcotics addict because you do not have strong motivations in the other direction. Junk wins by default.

I tried it as a matter of curiosity. I drifted along taking shots when
I could score. I ended up hooked. Most addicts I have talked to
report a similar experience. They did not start using drugs for any
reason they can remember. They just drifted along until they got
hooked. If you have never been addicted, you can have no clear idea
what it means to need junk with the addict's special need.
You don't decide to be an addict. One morning you wake up sick
and you're an addict.[62]

— *William Burroughs, Junkie*

In a widely circulated account of the contemporary heroin epidemic in *New York Magazine*, Andrew Sullivan gave one of the most compelling journalistic readings of this devastating crisis. Sullivan locates the roots of this crisis precisely where it is: as a socialized pathology that has emerged in direct response to the rise of digital technologies and globalized capitalism, both of which have exploded into our social, cultural, and biological spaces over the past decades. This is the combination — a globalized capitalism that has become fully synchronized with computational technologies — that has endlessly proliferated throughout all corners of American life while causing untold damage, not just to the local economies of communities across the country, but to the very emotional and psychic terrain of America itself:

The poppy's power, in fact, is greater than ever. The molecules derived from it have effectively conquered contemporary

America. Opium, heroin, morphine, and a universe of other synthetic opioids, including the super powerful painkiller fentanyl, are its proliferating offspring. More than 2 million Americans are now hooked on some kind of opioid, and drug overdoses - from heroin and fentanyl in particular- claimed more American lives last year than were lost in the entire Vietnam War. Overdose deaths are higher than in the peak year of AIDS and far higher than fatalities from car crashes. The poppy, through its many off shoots, has now been responsible for a decline of life spans in America for two years in a row, a decline that isn't happening in any other developed nation. According to the best estimates, opioids will kill another 52,000 Americans this year alone - and up to a half million in the next decade.[63]

But where Sullivan is at his best is when he contrasts the modern surge in opiate use with a similar moment that occurred in Britain in the late 19th century. The early development of industrialized capitalism, a development that drew countless rural individuals and families away from their traditional pastoral lives into the teeming cities of a rapidly modernizing England — the cities of factories, warehouses, and docks that were central to 19th century economies — also brought with it an existential crisis of its own, a crisis of meaning for the new urban transplants that interestingly enough gave way to an explosion of opioid abuse in its own right.

And in many ways we can locate the contemporary version of this crisis in America as the precise obverse of the one that took place in 19th century Britain: where the first opiate crisis was caused by the rise of industrialization, the second is caused by its very collapse; where the first opiate crisis was given particular form by the traumatized rural peasants forced to become accustomed to the rhythm of the factory in lieu of the rhythm of the sun, moon, and the seasons; the second crisis is being caused by the rhythm of the factory being outsourced by the rhythm of the smartphone. Or, to be more precise: the haunting fact that the postindustrial economy is absent a rhythm of its own; we now live in the age of "real time."

Sullivan locates the paradox of this situation perfectly:

As small armies of human beings were lured from their accustomed rural environments, with traditions and seasons and community, and thrown into vast new industrialized cities, the psychic stress gave opium an allure not even alcohol could match. Some historians estimate that as much as 10 percent of a working family's income in industrializing Britain was spent on opium. By 1870, opium was more available in the United States than tobacco was in 1970. It was as if the shift toward modernity and a wholly different kind of life for humanity necessitated for most working people some kind of relief — some way of getting out of the train while it was still moving.

It is tempting to wonder if, in the future, today's crisis will be seen as generated from the same kind of trauma, this time in reverse. If industrialization caused an opium epidemic, deindustrialization is no small part of what's fueling our opioid surge. It's telling that the drug has not taken off as intensely among all Americans — especially not among the engaged, multiethnic, urban-dwelling, financially successful inhabitants of the coasts. The poppy has instead found a home in those places left behind — towns and small cities that owed their success to a particular industry, whose civic life was built around a factory or a mine. Unlike in Europe, where cities and towns existed long before industrialization, much of America's heartland has no remaining preindustrial history, given the destruction of Native American societies. The gutting of that industrial backbone — especially as globalization intensified in a country where market forces are least restrained — has been not just an economic fact but a cultural, even spiritual devastation.[64]

What Sullivan touches upon here is the monstrous truth that is now being unveiled by the heroin crisis in countless cities and towns across America, cities and towns that were once directly plugged into the industrialized economy that are no longer able to function in the era of neoliberal globalization. And the monstrous truth is that behind these collapsed factory towns — behind these formerly close knit towns where everyone once went to the gymnasium on Friday nights to proudly cheer on the high school basketball team in a display of community solidarity — what now lurks is *nothing but* capitalism. With that we come back to Mark Fisher again to hear his prophetic words:

Capitalism is what is left when beliefs have collapsed at the level of ritual or symbolic elaboration, and all that is left is the consumer-spectator, trudging through the ruins and the relics.[65]

When Alexis de Tocqueville — one of the first great chroniclers of America and American life in the new republic — wrote his reflections on America in the early 1800s, one of the things that was most fascinating to him was the novel relationship in American culture between religion and commerce, the seeming symmetry between an embedded religious morality and the day to day operation of a burgeoning national economy. What he saw in pre-industrialized 19th century America was almost the exact opposite of how religion was used in his native France; where it was seen by Enlightenment thinkers like himself as a tool of historical domination and oppression by a French nobility and the Catholic Church. Whereas in America, de Tocqueville observed that religion functioned in an entirely different way, running instead side by side with the interrelated principals of democratization and decentralization:

In France I had almost always seen the spirit of religion and the spirit of freedom pursuing courses diametrically opposed

to each other, but in America I found that they were intimately united, and that they reigned in common over the same country.

Religion ... must be regarded as the foremost of the political institutions of the country for if it does not impart a taste for freedom, it facilitates the use of free institutions.[66]

de Tocqueville is essentially highlighting the differential between the medieval Catholic order and the emergent Protestant-inspired free market capitalism that was rapidly spreading across Europe and North America.

The true spirit of Capitalism, as Max Weber has noted, was intimately bound up with the Protestant ethos, an ethos that was fully exemplified by the original Puritan settlers of New England and was then passed down to successive generations as the original template of American business: hard work, self sufficiency, God helps those who help themselves, etc. Even as late as mid 20th century corporate American culture, we can see traces of this original dynamic still operative, as represented by the figure of the "gray suited man" who kept this link alive in his symbolic function: that there was an intimate relationship between the operation of American business and the Judeo-Christian moral fiber of western society.

But what has happened in recent years, as markets have transformed into their networked and digitized phase, is that capitalism has become increasingly rapacious, bare, and missing a symbolic screen to minimally mitigate its impact upon social life. It is now simply capitalism *as such*: abstract algorithms, indiscriminate computational processes, artificial intelligence, etc. The small towns and cities that dot the diverse topography of America have been completely and utterly stripped of this historical legacy that de Tocqueville referenced by these new globalizing and technical forces.[67] If religion even exists in America today it is in the primarily in the form of the evangelical mega-churches — which, far from addressing the socioeconomic pathologies of neoliberal globalization, endlessly exacerbates them. What this means is that part and parcel of the heroin crisis is an accompanying moral and spiritual blackout of the social terrain. Values such as community, land, and narrative — all qualities that have been absolutely central to the development of the countless unique localities throughout the various regions of America — are now openly disintegrating for corporate platforms, social media profiles, and the landless topographies of virtual space.

One can only note here the prophetic words of Marx when he spoke about the primitive nature of capitalism and how the global citizens of the 21st century, now fully mediated under what can only be called a "pure capitalism" increasingly absent any symbolic protection, are the ones who would live to see the bitter truth of Marx's fundamental insight:

The bourgeoisie, wherever it has got the upper hand, has put an end to all feudal, patriarchal, idyllic relations. It has pitilessly torn asunder the motley feudal ties that bound man to his 'natural superiors,' and has left remaining no other nexus between man and man than naked self-interest, callous 'cash payment.' It has drowned the most heavenly ecstasies of

religious fervor, of chivalrous enthusiasm, of philistine sentimentalism, in the icy water of egotistical calculation. It has resolved personal worth into exchange value, and in place of the numberless indefeasible chartered freedoms, has set up that single, unconscionable freedom—Free Trade. In one word, for exploitation, veiled by religious and political illusions, it has substituted naked, shameless, direct, brutal exploitation.[68]

The heroin crisis is ultimately a side effect of the bigger crisis of globalized capitalism in the 21st century. It is a crisis that runs directly alongside the "naked, shameless, direct, brutal exploitation" that defines the behavior of multinational corporations and the global media apparatus in the present age. We cannot sufficiently read the heroin crisis outside of this horizon, and any reading of this epidemic that tries to locate other causes — whether they be neuronal, social, geopolitical, etc. — as the root is simply unwilling to encounter what this crisis truly signifies. It is not so much that we are claiming globalized capitalism is "the cause" of heroin addiction. What we are rather saying is that all of the infinite causes that ultimately play their small part in creating each and every addict are all *mediated* by the objective violence[69] and ideological horizon of globalized capitalism itself.

Cultural Shifts

Every drug addiction, whether it be on the personal or cultural level, is always an attempt to reestablish a sense of homeostasis; to find the way back into a state of harmony from the past that is felt to have been irrevocably lost. Of course, as articulated in the field of psychoanalysis such a desire is a universal condition that extends far beyond the particularity of the addict's experience. It is a need that results from the "castration" that we experience as children, which thus allows for our entrance into the symbolic order.

But this universal sense of loss, which is undoubtedly the signature feature of the human condition as such, is absolutely radicalized in the life of the addict: each hit becomes a failed attempt to make contact with this mythical place where all pain and discomfort are nowhere to be found (i.e. to feel perfectly integrated into the symbolic order itself). And for the heroin addict specifically it is taken to another level of intensity and longing that is made visible by the drug's isolating, trance-like effect that results from the euphoria that is inscribed into the experience:

> **Heroin is the perfect drug for anyone who has been damaged by lack of self-esteem or traumatized by historical upheaval. It is the drug of battlefields, concentration camps, cancer wards, prisons, and ghettos. It is the drug of the resigned and the dissolute, the surely dying and the victims unwilling or unable to fight back.**[70]

What is interesting about the above quote, a passage taken from Terrance McKenna's 1992 book *Food of the Gods*, is the fact that even in 1992 McKenna — who was otherwise one of the most innovative and provocative writers of his generation on the relationship of a culture to its drugs — could not fathom that in the midst of his provocative list (concentration camps, battlefields, cancer wards, etc.) he would in the very near future have to include "suburban American homes surrounded by white picket fences." Even in 1992, less than ten years away from the start of the opiate epidemic that would indiscriminately sweep through American cities and towns across the country, McKenna was completely unable to locate the potentiality of such a drug to transcend the boundaries of the "ghetto" and metastasize throughout the entirety of the social edifice.

But what is perhaps most interesting about the passage is that even if McKenna is completely blind to the gestating potential of heroin to emerge as the universal drug of America in the 21st century, he nevertheless pinpoints the very reason for its explosive reach when he says that it is the perfect drug "for anyone who has been damaged by lack of self-esteem or traumatized by historical upheaval."

What could produce, in a directly lived experience, more of an effect in collectively destroying the self-esteem of an entire generation of Americans than the neoliberal horizon being applied to their daily experience? And furthermore, what could cause more "historical upheaval" than the various "shock treatments" that were put in place around the world to legitimize the neoliberal order (Chile and Russia in its more direct and brutal form; the US and the European Union in its diffuse application over time)[71] throughout all of our public and political spaces?

This is perhaps the missing link that we always overlook when we try to think about heroin addiction as both an individual and social pathology in the 21st century. And the reason why we miss it, time after time, is that we are fully enveloped in the ideological horizon that provided the very groundwork for this crisis to emerge. In other words, we can't conceive a political solution to this crisis — or even conceive as to what it actually signifies on the level of collective meaning — precisely because our critical reasoning capacity is colored by the problem itself. How can we locate the neoliberal roots to the heroin epidemic if our entire way of life is now directly mediated by those same roots?

The genius of McKenna's insight, although not fully elaborated in his own vision, is that mainstream, bread and butter Americana — as in a suburb of Boston or a small town in Indiana or Michigan — is now being progressively "ghetto-ized" in its own right within the early decades of the 21st century. The question thus becomes: how could McKenna possibly miss such a phenomenon that was so close to becoming reality?[72] How could he correctly theoretically link the relationship between trauma, the "ghetto" experience, and heroin and yet totally overlook that there was a whole new kind of "ghetto" on the verge of emerging in American society?

McKenna died not long after the publication of this same passage we have concentrated on, so he was never able to see his theory of heroin gain an entirely new dimension and demographic. The point here maybe is the fact that with McKenna writing in San Francisco in the early 1990s — surrounded by the techno-utopian visions that were then emanating out of Silicon Valley virtually every day at the time, surrounded by and embedded into the so called progressive political matrix of the greater Bay Area — the emergent reality of the Other America as a potential hotspot for heroin addiction would have been impossible to even conceive of it. But the fact of the matter is that the 1990s — the decade in which Oxycontin would be released onto the market, the pharmacological precursor to the heroin crisis — was perhaps the critical decade in which the roots of the heroin crisis would burrow itself deep into the American psyche.

Heroin as A Mirror of Public Space

When the collective perception of a certain drug is perceived as emblematic to a particular time period — "Everyone is doing heroin these days" — it is not simply a contingent feature of the historical period in question, it rather speaks to something essential about the very contingency itself. For instance, to claim that cocaine was America's "drug of choice" in the 1980s is far from a factual statement that speaks to a formal sociological reality. However, the very enunciation of such an ambiguous, empirically loose claim nevertheless retroactively opens the space to perceive how the energetic properties of cocaine were in fact deeply homologous to the greater socioeconomic forces of that decade: the homology spoke to the conditions of the 1980s in which cocaine appeared in a close symbolic relation.

To be more precise: it is now clear that the emergence of neoliberalism that suddenly presented itself as the only game in town for Western economies — the Reagan/Thatcher led program of breaking down the welfare state, union power, and the longstanding postwar compact between labor and capital in favor of mass privatization and direct market access[73] — and the dramatic emergence of Columbian cocaine crossing the southern American border shared in a certain ideological texture. The sensory rush produced by a line of quality cocaine — a sudden burst of dis-regulated energy, flows of chemical agents that engender a spontaneous frenzy to countless neurons sending the user into a hyperactive state occasionally bordering on mania — was perhaps articulated as the drug that best symbolized the cultural conditions of the 1980s because its qualities provided an adequate metaphor for America turning on MTV for the first time, Gordon Gecko emerging as the archetypal Wall Street figure unabashedly stating that "greed is good, greed is right, greed works," and the sheer excitement that accompanied the early stages of the "solid" social compositions that defined the industrial economy melting away for more flexible and self-created possibilities.[74]

Cocaine is the drug of Wall Street traders suddenly encountering a global market that is being both rapidly deregulated and linked into vast electronic networks of communication. Cocaine is the drug of young urban professionals who encounter the bright lights of the big city no longer defined by working class, close-knit ethnically mediated neighborhoods. And cocaine is the drug of a society feeling the potential for what lay ahead in a world that was suddenly starting to spin faster than it ever had before: with cocaine, one felt that they could keep up with the mounting velocity of time and space.

The two primary physiological effects of cocaine are that it is both an anesthetic and a stimulant.[75] That is to say, it causes the user to simultaneously experience both a sense of numbness and a sense of mania at the same time. Such a combination was a near perfect match for what was required to thrive in the 1980s, which is precisely why throughout that decade cocaine was ideologically presented as "the drug of choice." The anesthetic component of cocaine was necessary to block out all feeling, any ethical sense that may have posed serious questions in regard to the situation that was in the process of developing, whereas the stimulant component was necessary to keep pace with the increasing speed of global markets and the microelectronic technologies that were then being developed in Silicon Valley.

However, the feeling of excitement that defined the neoliberal turn and the happy 1980s — socioeconomic and ideological forces akin to the *zing* brought forth by a line of cocaine — is no longer a sufficient metaphor that is able to effectively symbolize the quality of 21st century American life: the genuine cultural enamor with MTV videos in the 1980s has become the overbearing weight of 24/7 social media feeds, the sheer banality of endless viral videos that have brought forth a profound neuronal lethargy rather than curiosity;[76] and, in equal measure, the legendary Wall Street escapades of the 1980s do not even compare to the raw power of global markets in their integrated, algorithmic contemporary form.

Such a scenario is perhaps why a drug like heroin — or any opiate for that matter — is currently *en vogue,* and why cocaine has in many ways receded to the cultural background. Cocaine is simply not able to adequately capture in its symbolic chain of meaning the conditions of our collective digital experience.

If the individual is now overwhelmed by the intersection of digital technologies, raw Capital deployment into our public and social spaces, along with rampant cultural globalization, then heroin — in stark opposition to a *stimulating* drug like cocaine — has perhaps risen to such an epidemic level because its affective properties rather act as a *depressive* screen to help mitigate against the consequences of such information overload in our psychic economy. In so many ways, the effects of opiates ultimately serve as a temporary calming agent to society's perpetually activated nervous system:

The digital network is provoking an intensification of the info-stimuli, and these are transmitted from the social brain to the individual brains. The acceleration is a pathogenic factor that has wide ranging effects in society.[77]

Widespread heroin addiction in the 21st century — although becoming so culturally visible in the present from a variety of factors that range from macro global issues such as failed border security to micro social issues such as the ongoing collapse of the family structure —- is ultimately a *specific kind* of addiction that should be gauged in all of its symbolic weight. The transmutation of global capitalism in the 1970s and 1980s; dislocating itself from fixed sites of production, waged labor, and then discarding a host of basic social protections that were once central to the embedded liberalism of mid-20th century American capitalism have now morphed into a virtualized, financially based contemporary form.[78]

Such a truly profound transformation of the economy has thus engaged the individual in a way in which he or she is not able to sufficiently adjust; the severity and violence of its endless neurological demands, its "everyman for himself" core ideological axiom are simply *too much* for the majority of people to effectively assimilate. The ongoing digitization and privatization of culture has made all things available at the touch of a keyboard, and the effect is a severely overstimulated collective nervous system that becomes relegated to a near constant state of intense craving: by using heroin, one is moved to the last resort of mitigating the mania and aggression of this information overload on the already taxed out psyche.

We can see, from a different perspective, this same ideological disjuncture — cocaine in the 1980s symbolizing the emergence of the neoliberal model and its unbounded promises; heroin in the second decade of the 21st century symbolizing a way to cope with those very same promises being unveiled for their emptiness — in the far more violent example between the heroin epidemic in the suburban present and the crack cocaine scourge in 1980s African-American inner city neighborhoods. The heroin crisis, as it has spilled out into the suburbs destroying countless families from the effect of overdoses and fatalities, has become an important topic of public discourse: it is perceived as a highly visible issue of social concern that has mobilized an entire generation of middle class American parents as they have helplessly watched their children encounter the violent reality of opiate addiction even within the historically safe confines of white picket fences. The public discourse surrounding heroin has not been one of strictly blanket criminalization, but also of understanding, compassion, while in many cases attempting to reform the entire *modus operandi* of the addict/police relationship as well as the very stigma often associated with drug addiction.[79]

However, throughout the 1980s, this same kind of social awareness was by no means extended to the inner city, overwhelmingly African American communities that were undergoing a narcotic crisis of their own. Crack cocaine — an explosive, ultra-violent drug that is in many ways diametrically opposed to the affective content of opiates — was seen by greater American society almost exclusively in its criminal dimensions: its public discourse was that of a drug associated with the black urban underclass; and, a drug that was *not in the suburbs.*[80]

The following summarizes the dimensions of this historical disjuncture:

That Kroger, the Midwestern grocery chain, has decided to make the heroin overdose drug naloxone available without a prescription is a sign of how ominous the current epidemic has grown.

Faced with a rising wave of addiction, misery, crime and death, our nation has linked arms to save souls. Senators and CEOs, Midwestern pharmacies and even tough-on-crime Republican presidential candidates now speak with moving compassion about the real people crippled by addiction.

It wasn't always this way. Thirty years ago, America was facing a similar wave of addiction, death and crime, and the response could not have been more different. Television brought us endless images of thin, black, ravaged bodies,

always with desperate, dried lips. We learned the words crack baby.

Back then, when addiction was a black problem, there was no wave of national compassion. Instead, we were warned of super predators, young, faceless black men wearing bandannas and sagging jeans.

No matter how far from our lives crack was, we're guilty by association. By the time I was in college in the early 1990s, my short dreadlocks meant older women would cross the street to avoid me.

African-Americans were cast as pathological. Their plight was evidence of collective moral failure, of welfare mothers and rock-slinging thugs and a reason to cut off all help. Blacks would just have to pull themselves out of the crack epidemic. Until then, the only answer lay in cordoning off the wreckage with militarized policing. One former narcotics officers said: "These are people. They have a purpose in life, and we can't look at it any other way."

But he couldn't quite put his finger on just what had changed. His words reflect our collective self-denial. It is hard to describe how bittersweet many African-Americans feel witnessing this. Glad to be rid of a failed war on drugs? Yes, but also weary and embittered. When the faces of addiction had dark skin, the police didn't see sons and daughters,

sister and brothers. They saw brothas, young thugs to be locked up, not people with a purpose in life.[81]

Jamarhl Crawford, an activist and writer based in the Roxbury neighborhood of Boston — the traditional African-American community of the city — has been an outspoken voice in his community who has written and spoken against not only the cumulative effects of something like gentrification in the present moment — a force that is now noticeably beginning to displace many African American residents from the Roxbury neighborhood — but also a voice that has not forgotten the social trauma of the postwar era that he and his community so painfully experienced. He notes the incredible hypocrisy of the differentiated responses that the crack cocaine epidemic — in which an entire generation of young black men were handed down lengthy prison sentences, many for non-violent offenses — and the emerging public discourses that the contemporary heroin epidemic has generated from social authority that has instead placed a premium on understanding, treatment, and prevention:

Where were all the rehab centers in Roxbury back in the 70s and 80s? There were plenty actually, they were called prisons … Soon as the white suburban kid gets hooked on heroin, our whole country, all the politicians start scrambling around for answers like chickens with their heads cut off. But that didn't happen here {in Roxbury} back then. They just put us in jail instead.[82]

There can be no doubt that Crawford's comments reference racism in its most obvious, and painful dimensions. However, it is important to note what also differentiates the drastically different societal response between the heroin epidemic in the present and the crack cocaine epidemic in the 1980s. Crack cocaine freely circulating within urban American space in the 1980s signified the "rock bottom" of the urban American deindustrialization process, the hollowing out of the City's former economic potential that had such drastic consequences for the African American community; especially those members of the Great Migration that had wagered their northern relocation on the very hopes of a thriving industrial economy and the social protections not available in the South.[83] In this very sense, the crack cocaine epidemic of the 1980s was the representation of a social ***explosion***: reflective of the ultra-insularity, violence, and the visible retreat of postwar City residents further and further into their already decomposing urban communities. Whereas on the other hand the profound cultural visibility of the contemporary heroin epidemic is rather reflective of the emerging dislocation of world Capital from time and place; a reference to the psychic and cultural effects that globalization is having on human communities. Contemporary heroin addiction thus functions in a way that is akin to a "viral video," an epidemic that effortlessly extends itself across borders, socioeconomic backgrounds, and particular cultural categories as it proliferates into the cellular make-up of American society. Heroin, today, in stark contrast to crack cocaine, is reflective of a social ***implosion***: the inability of the social body, and its brain, to sufficiently integrate the effects of virtualized capitalism and the cultural ramifications of constant digital exposure.

Purdue Pharma, Oxycontin, and Heroin

To understand the heroin crisis of 2018, it is necessary to trace it back to the Oxycontin crisis that preceded it; to clearly perceive the direct link between a refined, laboratory produced pharmacological compound that was released into consumer markets in the mid-1990s under the brand-name Oxycontin and the explosion of illegal street heroin that followed a decade later.

But before we even begin we already run into a problem, by not sufficiently recognizing that when heroin itself was first synthesized in the late 1800's by a German chemist[84] it too was considered a refined, laboratory produced pharmacological compound. What we see here is somewhat of a false dichotomy in the narrative between Oxycontin and heroin: Oxycontin is perceived as a refined, synthetic pharmaceutical whereas street heroin is seen almost "naturalized," a more authentic and raw version of an opiate than its laboratory produced counterpart. This false dichotomy rather speaks to the "naturalization" function that a culture grants to any technology or product once it has been sufficiently integrated into its social-symbolic order: the seeming "natural" quality of heroin as opposed to the purely synthetic Oxycontin is simply a derivative of time itself.

But all hair splitting aside, to really grasp the contemporary heroin crisis, we must first encounter Oxycontin and the company that produced it.

Where the fascinating history of Purdue Pharma, the privately owned company that developed Oxycontin, and the three brothers — Arthur, Raymond, and Mortimer Sackler — who transformed this small, unknown drug firm into a billion dollar pharmaceutical giant ultimately rests is not so much in creating drugs, but in *creating brands*:

The richest newcomer to Forbes 2015 list of America's Richest Families comes in at a stunning $14 billion. The Sackler family, which owns Stamford, Conn.-based Purdue Pharma, flew under the radar when Forbes launched its initial list of wealthiest families in July 2014, but this year they crack the top-20, edging out storied families like the Busches, Mellons and Rockefellers.

How did the Sacklers build the 16th-largest fortune in the country? The short answer: making the most popular and controversial opioid of the 21st century — OxyContin.

Purdue, 100% owned by the Sacklers, has generated estimated sales of more than $35 billion since releasing its time-released, supposedly addiction-proof version of the painkiller oxycodone back in 1995. Its annual revenues are about $3 billion, still mostly from OxyContin. The Sacklers also own separate drug companies that sell to Asia, Latin America, Canada and Europe, together generating similar total sales as Purdue's operation in the United States.[85]

What this means, and as implicitly alluded to in the above passage, is that the multi-billion dollar success of Purdue and its signature drug Oxycontin was not necessarily due to some profound scientific breakthrough in the field of pain management; it was rather an exercise in marketing genius, and *perfect timing*: the Oxycontin moment that began at the close of the 20th century was also the moment when existent social and cultural conditions produced a situation in which a desperate need for self-regulation — through euphoria, dissociation, and detachment — began to surface in the collective brain of American society. The Clinton era, the dot com boom — the so called "Prozac economy" of the 1900s[86] — was a time when the forces of digital technology and neoliberal globalization would collide and engender a profound spiritual and social void in American culture, a void in which the entrance of Oxycontin onto the market, and then in its function as an illegal street drug, would move to fill.

But long before the Sackler brothers became pharmaceutical industry executives in their own right through the purchase of the struggling, one hundred year old Manhattan based pharmaceutical firm Purdue Fredrick[87]— in which they would eventually transform it into the multi-billion conglomerate known as Purdue Pharma and create drugs such as Oxycontin — they had *already* made a small fortune in the pharmaceutical industry: not as executives of another drug firm, but as industry leaders in the burgeoning, postwar field of pharmaceutical marketing and advertising. The Sacklers — the men who founded the company that brought the world Oxycontin in 1996— can be effectively described as the original

"Mad Men" of the postwar drug industry. Arthur Sackler, the oldest of the three brothers, virtually invented pharmacological advertising in its modern form.[88]

The pharmaceutical advertising company Sackler ran in the 1940s, the Manhattan based William Douglas McAdams, was where these brothers would hone and perfect their innovative marketing and advertising techniques. Here, at the pharmaceutical industry's exterior — as an outside advertising consultant able to apprehend the workings of an entire industry — the Sackler run advertising firm would assist some of the largest pharmaceutical corporations in the world, position an entire catalogue of novel drugs onto the American market for the very first time, aptly demonstrated in its pivotal role bringing Librium and Valium to the public:

Arthur Sackler not only paved new ways for marketing drugs, he helped create a new chapter in American life— the emergence of the pill as a quick fix ... it was Arthur Sackler's marketing genius that turned Librium and Valium into not only the greatest pharmaceutical successes of their era but also medicine chest and nightstand drawer staples throughout the United States. Pharmacologically, Librium and Valium belonged to the same class of drugs, the benzodiazepines; they worked similarly to calm a patient's nerves, and both were potentially addicting. But Arthur, working as a consultant to the drugs' producer, Hoffman-LaRoche of

Switzerland, skillfully promoted them as though they were two entirely different medications so that doctors would use them for different problems and the two products would not cannibalize each other's sales. He positioned Librium, which was launched first, as a treatment for "anxiety" while promoting Valium for a separate set of mental concerns and preoccupations that he defined as "psychic tension." Using that battle plan, Roche Labs, Hoffman-LaRoche's subsidiary in the United States, spent between $ 150 million and $200 million during the 1960s to promote its twin tranquilizers, a level of spending never before seen in the pharmaceutical industry.[89]

Can we not see in the above passage — two chemically similar drugs manufactured by the same multinational pharmaceutical firm that are then branded and marketed by the Sackler firm to create two entirely distinct markets — traces of the Oxycontin narrative beginning to flower? Such a backstory to the history of Purdue Pharma points to why the catastrophe of Oxycontin 40 years later should be paid careful attention to: the architects of Oxycontin were not simply the architects of Oxycontin, but were key figures in the modern formation of the entire pharmaceutical industry. The Sackler brothers were instrumental in creating, not strictly Purdue Pharma or Oxycontin, but the contemporary pharmaceutical industry *as such*, in all of its marketing and branding excesses. This is why we can be fairly suspicious that when Oxycontin was continually presented to doctors around the country through Purdue's highly sophisticated informational and marketing apparatus — in which Oxycontin was discoursed in scientifically neutral terms as a safe, effective medication for pain management with minimal addictive potential — Purdue, as has been thoroughly documented, knew full well the extent of the damage this product was creating in communities around the country, and denied it nonetheless.[90]

Such marketing trickery in the pharmaceutical industry is nothing new. Ever since the early 19th century, with the expanding market of a variety of opiate based syrups and elixirs designed to alleviate pain and calm the nerves, "innovative" marketing and advertising techniques were employed in order to sell the product more efficiently to the public:

Advertising became more innovative. Patent medicine companies distributed collectible trading cards beginning in the 1820s and peaking in the 1880s. Early examples showed peaceful rural or historical scenes; the later ones pulled off the gloves: Mrs. Winslow's issued a series of chromolithographs featuring loving mothers soaking their babies in alcohol and morphine sulfate ... And that was just the start; brand names were painted in letters several feet high on the side of barns; men sporting sandwich boards walked city streets; promotional merchandise such as Monell's Teething Syrup clocks was distributed to druggists; and itinerant quacks, regularly hopping from town to town, skillfully roped in suckers.[91]

In the postwar era, the American pharmaceutical industry seemed to put an end to such obvious quackery easily discernible in the early forms of marketing and advertising in the 19th and early 20th centuries. But, and as clearly demonstrated in the case of Purdue Pharma and the national opiate epidemic they unleashed from their signature product Oxycontin, the quackery was nevertheless stronger than ever. That is to say, the peer reviewed, scientific evidence that Purdue distributed to doctors around the country to justify the millions of prescriptions that were written for Oxycontin was clearly nothing but a sophisticated marketing ploy, a contemporary version of "men sporting sandwich boards walking across city streets." When Russel Portenoy, the chief scientist for Purdue Pharma, wrote in an issue of the medical journal *Pain*, "We conclude that opiod maintenance therapy can be a safe … and more humane alternative to the options of surgery or no treatment in those patients with intractable non-malignant pain and no history of drug abuse,"[92] such a comment can now be viewed retroactively as being akin to a man wearing a sandwich board selling elixirs on a 19th century street corner.

But the apparent safety that Portenoy and Purdue Pharma touted to doctors around the country regarding Oxycontin ended up creating a situation that was *anything* but safe:

A 2016 report issued by the San Francisco, California based health care consulting company Castlight Health found that in 2012 doctors wrote 259 million prescriptions for opiod painkillers – nearly enough prescriptions to provide every

American with his or her own bottle of pills. Moreover, a CDC report found that in some states, there are more opiod prescriptions than there are people. In 2012 in Alabama and Tennessee, for example, the CDC reported that there were about 143 opiod prescriptions written for every 100 people.[93]

But, ultimately, it was not simply Purdue's marketing acumen, or even their blatant distortion of Oxycontin's explosive addictive potential that was solely responsible for this epidemic to have materialized throughout society so effortlessly. What we can rather see in the origins of this epidemic is the systemic nature of an entire industry: drug firms looking for higher profits, insurers looking to cut costs, pressures from investors, and patient advocacy groups funded by pharmaceutical firms demanding access to powerful pain medications:

The boom in opioid use is a direct result of the forces that were set into motion in the late 1990s when the "War on Pain" began. Drug makers such as Purdue Pharma aggressively promoted newer and stronger drugs to doctors who were unfamiliar with their use, the treatment of chronic pain or substance abuse. Insurers, through their reimbursement policies, guaranteed that narcotics would become the predominant treatment for chronic pain. Lobbying groups and patient advocacy organizations, many of them with financial

ties to the drug industry, succeeded in changing state laws to make it easier for doctors to prescribe narcotics without fear of sanctions ...Insurers embraced opioids because their immediate cost – the price of pills – was lower than alternative approaches such as multidisciplinary treatment programs. Treating a patient with an opioid like OxyContin costs about $ 6,000 a year while putting the same patient through a comprehensive pain program can run from $ 15,000 to $25,000.[94]

However, what is notoriously missing from the above passage, a passage that otherwise offers an accurate summary of the underlying network that incubated the Oxycontin epidemic, is the fact of an entire society reaching a proverbial breaking point. Contra to the thesis in the above passage, the boom in opiod use was *not* strictly "set in motion in the late 1990s" by factors within the pharmaceutical industry itself, or the specific actions of Purdue Pharma. The explosive increase in opiod use at the turn of the century in American society was also deeply related to the ongoing deterioration of social life, the exponential decline of our collective psychological health, and the continuing dumbing-down of American culture. The deregulation of markets, the truly shocking privatization of public space, the decomposing status of the family unit and the local community — these factors and more, all catalyzed and accelerated by the diverse procedures of globalization that had already appeared more than two decades prior —must be taken into account to produce a sufficient narrative of the Oxycontin epidemic.

⚔

The opiate crisis, perhaps more than any other pressing socioeconomic issue in present day American society, cuts right to the very heart of the contemporary global order. But not only does it cut to the heart of the matter, it is a topic of conversation that people will actually shut up and listen to. People will listen to *anything* that attempts to coherently and honestly explain the roots of this issue because it is an issue that has personally affected so many.

Would not a Donald Trump supporting parent of a heroin addict and a Hillary Clinton supporting parent of a heroin addict, when hearing legitimate critique and analysis about the roots of this crisis, be willing to sit side by side in the same room and actually agree on something if it were to help their children?

I know of no other issue in contemporary American society that has such an explosive potential to be a source of universal thinking that directly addresses the operation of globalized capitalism in the present moment. It is a crisis that carries with it a potential that can cut directly across any and all of the apparent divides — political, social, or cultural — that are now dangerously developing in American society. In this precise sense, the contemporary heroin addict is as close to a version of the modern day proletariat, a social agent that can be the bearer of *universality*; the "part of no part" that can nevertheless stand in for and represent the universal as such.

Neoliberal Healing

What I wish to explore is how social justice and environmental issues could be addressed through sustainable business solutions that are profitable. It is this intersection of "economics-humanity-sustainability" that I wish to explore. Whether you think of pressing issues such as refugee crisis, gender inequality, or plastic pollution in the ocean — I believe that sustainable business models can provide long term solutions (through job creation, equal employment opportunity, eco-friendly packaging and supply chain decisions, etc.)

In my experience, very little is achieved through conventional charity, activism, or analytics alone. Without inherent economic impetus long-term change in mass scale is not possible. In conjunction, policy advocacy to create the fundamental framework to promote such innovative ecosystems is absolutely critical at this point of time. So, I came here to surround myself with brilliant minds and to reinforce my aspiration to become a "change agent" in my own little

humble way.[95]

— *Facebook post*

T̲he key strategy of neoliberalism in dealing with the truly explosive potential of the American heroin crisis has been to endlessly "privatize" the
suffering of the addict: to reduce the suffering into that of a neurological
dysfunction, a particular pathology rooted within the network of opiod
receptors in the Central Nervous System; or, as the result of a biographical trauma that has manifested in something like PTSD in which addiction serves as a means of self-medication. In either case, no matter the
underlying causal chain — whether it is reduced into a purely neuronal
formula or if it is seen as a psychological symptom — neoliberalism
regards opiod addiction as a process that can be sufficiently addressed
through a model of technical intervention and privatized therapy: as in
pharmaceutical drugs such as Methadone, Buprenorphine, or Narcan;[96]
or from the various methodologies now central to the private rehabilitation centers emerging across the country to address this epidemic. In
other words, perhaps the principal drive behind the passion to arrest
this epidemic — a passion that we can even see emanating from the
office of the President of the United States as Donald Trump has made
numerous references to the reality of heroin addiction and its devastating effect on American communities throughout his 2016 campaign
and into his Presidential term[97] — is to frame the problem of heroin

addiction as something that the market itself should first and foremost address.

Case in point is the New York City start-up Groups, whose surreal motto is, "Community, Fellowship, and Buprenorphine deliver superior results." Groups could be effectively characterized as the neoliberal, "2.0 version" of something like Alcoholics Anonymous: a private start-up that is based around the combination of supervised weekly group therapy meetings supplemented with Buprenorphine treatment:

> **Groups is meeting the epidemic head-on. The unprecedented scale of opioid abuse requires a new way to treat this disease. We are a for-profit medical practice because it's the best way to bring this solution to the most people possible. To confine this work to the realm of government and charity means we will never catch up, forever one step behind.**
>
> **We know what works. It's time to act.**[98]

Although it might be true that such a platform may in fact be helpful to many addicts amidst the desperation of the present situation, it should also be noted that what such a business model ultimately does is to completely block the inherent *political* and *public* dimension of this crisis. Such naked privatization erects a near insurmountable obstacle so that the "private suffering" of the addict cannot be translated into a political mobilization and a public reckoning.

The problem we encounter here with a private start-up like Groups is the fact that the 21ˢᵗ century heroin scourge throughout American society is the very definition of a public crisis: it is the very definition of a gestating political moment. In other words: *heroin addiction is political.*

Perhaps the key function of neoliberalism is how it progressively collapses all public space. The drive towards privatization within the horizon of neoliberalism is nearly absolute, it is a drive embedded into the very core of the neoliberal project since its earliest mobilization.[99] From public education, to public transportation, to public utilities, to even our public conversations that now occurs on the various social medias mined by algorithms for potentially valuable data so as to further build our consumer profiles. The absolute obscenity of this system, a system in which the charged discourses of privatization have now become neutralized through ideology, is perfectly satirized by the Portuguese novelist Jose Saramago in the following passage:

Privatize everything, privatize the sea and the sky, privatize the water and the air, privatize justice and the law, privatize the passing cloud, privatize the dream, especially if it's during the day and open eyed. And finally, for the embellishment of so many privatizations, privatize the States, surrender once and for all their exploitation to private companies through international share offering. There lies the salvation of the world.[100]

The contemporary heroin addict is perhaps the elementary example of this "privatization" as a derivative from the ongoing disintegration of public spaces, local communities, and our collective psychic vitality by the one-two punch of global markets and global technology: the heroin addict is left to himself, and nothing more, to find his next hit. And, from the opposite perspective, the heroin addict is now left to herself, and nothing more, to get help as well. That is to say, the heroin addict exemplifies the core drive of this very system in both the drive of active addiction **and** the drive to heal from it.

When we speak of privatization we are not simply referring to public schools being handed over to for-profit charter schools to educate our children, or the once publicly owned and managed railways being sold at rock bottom prices to multinationals, we are also referring to the privatization of the very Self. The Self is by no means a "private" entity, even though it remains forever mysterious and inaccessible. The Self is fundamentally predicated on a series of exchanges with the Other, it is based upon an ongoing relation of language, sense, and experience with the Other.[101] But when the Self becomes "privatized" as it is today across both American and global society — that is to say, when it loses its ability to spontaneously relate to the Other without being directly mediated by a capitalist or technical medium — it becomes progressively traumatized, narcissistic, then finally implodes from the pressures of this ongoing privatization:

Today, we hear a great deal, but we are increasingly losing the ability to listen to Others and give an ear to their

language, to their suffering. Today, everyone is somehow on their own with themselves, with their suffering, with their fears. Suffering is privatized and individualized. Thus it becomes an object of therapy that tampers with the I, with its psyche. Everyone is ashamed and simply blames themselves for their weakness and inadequacy. No connection is established between my suffering and your suffering. The sociality of suffering is overlooked.[102]

The Self, when left alone, when regarded as itself and nothing more, has no choice within such a horizon but to become a strictly *homo economicus*: a social agent who is principally programmed to compete, produce, and achieve within the confines of a purely capitalist frame. But the spiritual degradation of human life under this system is now becoming staggering, and we can see it every day in no uncertain terms with the endless scandals of our politicians, the innocent teenage students being gunned down at their public high schools, the psychological violence of Reality Television confessionals, and in the experience of our young next door neighbor who is now a heroin junkie.

There is a crisis of the Self that is unfolding in perhaps unprecedented terms today, for the Self is "under siege" to put it in the terms of the late cultural critic Rick Roderick.[103] The Self is disintegrating even as its displays of narcissism and the most toxic kinds of self-aggrandizing behavior dominate the headlines of our culture. But such displays are fundamentally cries for recognition, they are desperate screams to be recognized by the Other. But as the Self is further privatized, as the Self is further put into a model whereby he or she exists in a horizon of purely capitalist and technical exchanges, the "Other" ceases to even be a reality.

But the presence of the Other is how we discover who we even are.

Alcoholics Anonymous Under Attack[104]

Alcoholics Anonymous, a program and fellowship that was founded in 1935 by Bill Wilson and Dr. Robert Smith[105] is fundamentally predicated upon the presence of the Other. That is to say, it is fundamentally based upon an active and suffering alcoholic entering into a living relationship with a recovered alcoholic, a person who has completed the program of recovery and is thus qualified to guide the active alcoholic/addict through the steps of recovery. It is essentially impossible to complete this program without the careful sponsorship of another human being, a fact that the founding literature of AA mentions again and again.

And then, beyond the particular relationship constituted by the alcoholic with his or her sponsor, there is also the relationship to the collective of the greater fellowship itself, which takes the shape of public meetings and group discussions that one can find virtually every night in church basements in cities around the world. In this precise sense, a program such as Alcoholics Anonymous is inherently "political," but absent any direct politicization: its primary "political" purpose is to bring the alcoholic/addict away from his or her self-destructive, narcissistic behavior and into a living relationship with the Other.

It is interesting to note how the inherent benevolence and simplicity of a spiritual program and public fellowship such as Alcoholics Anonymous — a kind of public program that is perhaps more relevant than ever today — has become the target of endless critique and ridicule by the neoliberal model of addiction recovery. It is derided for being hopelessly outdated, scientifically illiterate, and even delusional for basing part of its program on having the alcoholic/addict develop a relationship with a Higher Power (a fictitious God in their view) versus the discourses of contemporary cutting edge brain sciences, pharmaceutical interventions, and the recent literature from disciplines such as cognitive-behavioral therapy.

In a 2015 feature article in *Atlantic Magazine* entitled, "The Irrationality of Alcoholics Anonymous," we not only see this disdain openly revealed, but we also see such a critique's fundamental limitation, not to mention its very own brand of irrationality:

The 12 steps are so deeply ingrained in the United States that many people, including doctors and therapists, believe attending meetings, earning one's sobriety chips, and never taking another sip of alcohol is the only way to get better. Hospitals, outpatient clinics, and rehab centers use the 12 steps as the basis for treatment. But although few people seem to realize it, there are alternatives, including prescription drugs and therapies that aim to help patients learn to drink in moderation. Unlike Alcoholics Anonymous, these

methods are based on modern science and have been proved, in randomized, controlled studies, to work.[106]

The author is already confused, already missing the deeper point, that what constitutes an addict/alcoholic is not simply that they cannot safely use or drink under any circumstances, but the recognition that alcohol or drugs of any kind and in any quantity are detrimental to one's inner life. One cannot help but find a hidden kernel of neoliberal ideology here: what seems to bother the author so much is that part of the philosophy of AA is a complete end of drinking/using; that is to say, *a complete end of production/consumption*. The author's tone is frustrated, he wants people to realize that only if they took the right prescription medication, they could continue to indulge sporadically without the negative effects. In other words, from the viewpoint of this author, *you can continue to produce/consume without any repercussions*. Such a reading literally misses the entire point of what a program like AA even is.

The author continues his critique of AA in the following passage:

For a glimpse of how treatment works elsewhere, I traveled to Finland, a country that shares with the United States a history of prohibition (inspired by the American temperance movement, the Finns outlawed alcohol from 1919 to 1932) and a culture of heavy drinking.

Finland's treatment model is based in large part on the work of an American neuroscientist named John David

Sinclair ... Sinclair came to believe that people develop drinking problems through a chemical process: each time they drink, the endorphins released in the brain strengthen certain synapses. The stronger these synapses grow, the more likely the person is to think about, and eventually crave, alcohol—until almost anything can trigger a thirst for booze, and drinking becomes compulsive.

Sinclair theorized that if you could stop the endorphins from reaching their target, the brain's opiate receptors, you could gradually weaken the synapses, and the cravings would subside. To test this hypothesis, he administered opioid antagonists—drugs that block opiate receptors—to the specially bred alcohol-loving rats. He found that if the rats took the medication each time they were given alcohol, they gradually drank less and less. He published his findings in peer-reviewed journals beginning in the 1980s.

Subsequent studies found that an opioid antagonist called naltrexone was safe and effective for humans, and Sinclair began working with clinicians in Finland. He suggested prescribing naltrexone for patients to take an hour before drinking. As their cravings subsided, they could then learn to control their consumption. Numerous clinical trials have confirmed that the method is effective, and in 2001 Sinclair published a paper in the journal Alcohol and Alcoholism reporting a 78 percent success rate in helping patients reduce

their drinking to about 10 drinks a week. Some stopped drinking entirely.[107]

One can only marvel at the fact that this author has the audacity to frame Alcoholics Anonymous as an irrational, outdated program, yet sees no irrationality whatsoever in the fact that he is basing part of his thesis on a laboratory experiment that used "alcohol loving rats."

But of course, Sinclair is in fact correct in identifying the basic mechanism of any addiction, and that the way to arrest any addiction — whether it be heroin, alcohol, or any other substance — is to somehow stop the circular and self-reinforcing relationship of artificial endorphins binding to certain receptors in the brain.

No one reasonably educated in the field of addiction would ever deny the fact of a neurological base to addiction, no one would ever deny the brain as the key site of the addictive experience. However, one can deny, and one should push back forcefully, against the application of neoliberal ideology — under the guise of an uncontaminated, objective science — to a sick and suffering addict as a strategy to heal:

Bill Wilson, AA's founding father, was right when he insisted, 80 years ago, that alcohol dependence is an illness, not a moral failing. Why, then, do we so rarely treat it medically? It's a question I've heard many times from researchers and clinicians. "Alcohol- and substance-use disorders are the

realm of medicine," McLellan says. "This is not the realm of priests."[108]

Again, the author is absolutely correct to note that alcoholism (or substance abuse of any kind) is not the "realm of priests." But at the same time, is alcoholism (or addiction) the realm of rats, pharmacology, and venture capital backed start-ups? It most certainly is not. But this is the inherent blind spot that the author — whose theoretical address is unconsciously mediated by the neoliberal discourse— cannot sufficiently distinguish. For him it's either magical thinking or neoliberal science; it's either the realm of priests or the realm of rats. But this seeming "choice" that the author is presenting, this Either/Or, is not even a real choice, and in many ways it mirrors the false choice[109] that we are now constantly presented with in all nearly aspects of our culture. Under such a false predicament, we are now unable to see any real alternatives, we are now unable to even *imagine* any alternatives.

The position here is not to unilaterally defend a program such as AA and construct a blanket critique against any pharmacological or scientific intervention into the field of addiction recovery; to make the case that such interventions are stepping across the proper boundary of scientific inquiry and into the space of the purely human experience. Not at all. The point here is rather to note that these contemporary scientific interventions are by no means objectively neutral, that they are by no means that of an uncontaminated scientific discourse addressing this situation free from any ideological mediation. Quite the contrary, such interventions are fundamentally mediated by the ideological machinery of neoliberal, globalized capitalism and should be recognized as such.

It seems to be a matter of common sense that any heroin addict should necessarily possess a brain that is seriously inflamed from the use of such heavy narcotics, just as it is common sense that certain pharmaceutical drugs have been and are being developed to address such neural inflammation. But how this seeming simple correlation translates *in practice* is that part and parcel to the drive of both science and capitalism to somehow arrest this crisis is that these discourses must eventually reduce heroin addiction into that of a brain state — *and nothing more.* That is to say, to regard heroin addiction as a *private pathology* that is only in need of a "neutral" scientific address.

But such a position is *not* neutral, even as it desperately tries to present itself in such terms.

The main problem with such reductionist thinking — "addiction equals brain state and nothing more" — that is now becoming more and more common within the field of addiction recovery is not that such thinking misses so much of the addict's "actual lived experience and interiority," but rather that it distorts the potential to make an effective critique of the crisis itself. By shifting the discourses of addiction into the technical language of medical and scientific jargon, by transforming the potential to truly heal from the disease of addiction into a precise pharmacological formula, we are in a way losing what this epidemic may even signify on the social-symbolic level.

But this begs an even deeper question: if there ever was a pharmaco-logical "magic bullet" developed to completely cure addiction by a Silicon Valley biotechnology firm, would they even release its full potential to the public? That is to say, would such a "magic bullet" cure even be a viable business model to attract venture capital amidst the functioning of today's globalized capitalism? According to analysts at Goldman Sachs the answer to such an inquiry is a resounding *No*:

One-shot cures for diseases are not great for business—more specifically, they're bad for longer term profits—Goldman Sachs analysts noted in an April 10 report for biotech clients, first reported by CNBC.

The investment banks' report, titled "The Genome Revolution," asks clients the touchy question: "Is curing patients a sustainable business model?" The answer may be "no," according to follow-up information provided.

For a real-world example, they pointed to Gilead Sciences, which markets treatments for hepatitis C that have cure rates exceeding 90 percent. In 2015, the company's hepatitis C treatment sales peaked at $12.5 billion. But as more people were cured and there were fewer infected individuals to spread the disease, sales began to languish. Goldman Sachs analysts estimate that the treatments will bring in less than $4 billion this year.

"[Gilead]'s rapid rise and fall of its hepatitis C franchise highlights one of the dynamics of an effective drug that permanently cures a disease, resulting in a gradual exhaustion of the prevalent pool of patients," the analysts wrote. The report noted that diseases such as common cancers—where the "incident pool remains stable"—are less risky for business.

To get around the sustainability issue overall, the report suggests that biotech companies focus on diseases or conditions that seem to be becoming more common and/or are already high-incidence. It also suggests that companies be innovative and constantly expanding their portfolio of treatments.[110]

What we see here in no uncertain terms is the pathological core of neoliberal globalization when left to its own devices. The open brazenness of the analyst does not even attempt to shield itself behind the screen of any linguistic detour. What is revealed is simply point blank capitalism in all of its violence: why heal the patient when there is surplus value to be continually extracted from keeping him sick?

To reiterate, we should be absolutely open to any new scientific research and discovery regarding the biochemical or genetic roots of heroin addiction. But we should nevertheless take it all with a grain of salt, knowing full well that such research today is always-already mediated by a system that is first and foremost geared towards the reproduction of global capitalism in its current state.

What does such a position signified by this "neoliberal healing" model ultimately do? First and foremost it denies, it completely disavows, that something like heroin addiction could have a causation that is beyond the addict's neurological composition, that its roots could lie in the public field:

> The current ruling ontology denies any possibility of a social causation of mental illness. The chemico-biologization of mental illness is of course strictly commensurate with its de-politicization. Considering mental illness an individual chemico-biological problem has enormous benefits for capitalism. First, it reinforces Capital's drive towards atomistic individualization (you are sick because of your brain chemistry). Second, it provides an enormously lucrative market in which multinational pharmaceutical companies can peddle their pharmaceuticals (we can cure you with our SSRIs). It goes without saying that all mental illnesses are neurologically instantiated, but this says nothing about their causation. If it is true, for instance, that depression is constituted by low serotonin levels, what still needs to be explained is why particular individuals have low levels of serotonin. This requires a social and political explanation; and the task of re-politicizing mental illness is an urgent one if the left wants to challenge capitalist realism.[111]

The contemporary heroin addict — although most certainly a casualty of their own experience, personal choices, and neuronal composition — is also a casualty of the disintegration of our collective public life, public space, and community.[112] In order to fully address this crisis, in order to *heal* from this crisis, we must speak about both features of the addict's experience: the personal, neuronal, and spiritual; *and* the public, political, and cultural. They are interrelated, they fundamentally implicate and mirror each other. And speaking of one while denying the other can never lead to a true reckoning, to a true collective healing.

Virtual Recovery Communities

The logic of neoliberal healing, as applied to the recovery from heroin addiction, goes well beyond the continual elevation of the brain sciences and the reduction of heroin addiction to a "privatized pathology." It also extends into the very domain of community as well.

Recovery from something as ultra-violent as heroin addiction, *especially* when trying to accomplish such a feat while surrounded by a greater society such as ours, it is absolutely essential to discover our lost humanity: our capacity for empathy, humility, and basic decency; our capacity to recognize and listen to the voice of the Other. And for such a recovery to be actualized and embodied it has to happen as an ongoing practice in our day to day experience, in the direct experience of our flesh and its interdependence with nature, other bodies, and the greater symbolic chain of meaning that we always-already participate in.

In this very sense, the emergent model of "virtual recovery communities" — digital platforms that apply the basic logic of social media to the experience of recovery — are clearly symptomatic of the further ideological leakage of neoliberalism into the social domain. What virtual recovery communities are, at their elementary level, are simply entrepreneurial start-ups attempting to somehow monetize this crisis in the form of a website or app that provides a platform to appropriate its users' data for profit and shareholder value: about as diametrically opposed to the altruistic spirit of Alcoholics Anonymous as one can get. But, as recovery programs such as AA further descend into crisis from their inability to effectively respond to the ultra-utilitarian logic of globalized capitalism, such virtual recovery "communities" are proliferating in the fallout offering the potential of support to vulnerable addicts across the world.

What is interesting here is how clearly we can perceive the *objective violence* of neoliberal globalization.[113] That is to say, we can be rest assured that the people who have founded such websites and apps are by no means "bad people," that they are by no means subjectively malicious capitalists who are directly preying on a disenfranchised population. What is far more likely is that these entrepreneurs probably feel as if they are contributing to the betterment of society, that they have developed a solution to the very real crisis of the social isolation felt by addicts across the world.[114] They have been so passively indoctrinated by the ideological apparatus of neoliberal globalization that, to put it in the words of Christ in the Gospel of Luke, "Forgive them for they know not what they do."

A case in point that exemplifies where we can see this very mechanism being enacted is the social network and digital application Sober Grid, an app that was founded in 2014 as a platform of recovery resources. With over 100,000 active users today it is one of the largest of such recovery platforms in the world. The basic business model of Sober Grid is to capitalize upon, and then to technically organize into a network, the fact that the contemporary addict is first and foremost a solitary being: stripped from local community, local sensibility, and sociocultural bonds; that the contemporary addict is the free agent of contemporary social edifice *par excellence*. Sober Grid then presents itself as the neutral medium where these lost communal bonds can be relocated and reactivated in the context of an online recovery community.

It is, for all intents and purposes, the "Facebook" of the recovery world. But it is not so much that Sober Grid models itself after Facebook, *it is more the fact that Facebook models itself after Sober Grid.* Counter-intuitively, the basic logic of Facebook — the drive to transform human relationships into a algorithmic grid of pure technical and capitalist relations — actually rests upon the precise same principal as Sober Grid: that the contemporary individual, *regardless of whether they are an addict or not,* is now a solitary being: progressively stripped from local community, local sensibility, and sociocultural bonds, the 21st century global consumer is the free agent of the social edifice *par excellence*:

Facebook is an electronic neighborhood where virtual flaneurs can go strolling, saying "hello" to "friends," or else they just

try to convince themselves that other people do exist out there who are as lonely as they are. But the problem is that Facebook is a poor substitute for real human contact. It is a virtualization and replacement for the kinds of tangibility that human relations need in order to thrive and flourish. In coffee shops, after all, you can have long, interesting conversations with real friends. A great deal of European literature was worked out this way, in coffee shops such as the Café de la Regence or Café Procope (one of the very first) or Les Deux Magots in Paris, places frequented by the likes of Rousseau, Voltaire, Joyce, Picasso, Sartre, Henry Miller, etc ... But [Facebook's] very existence is a testament to the fact that communities and neighborhoods are disappearing everywhere from our maps.[115]

Such a passage tracing the underlying roots of Facebook is further confirmed in the copy from Sober Grid's own website regarding the basis of their product:

The sober community thrives on having a safe and supportive environment. Sober Grid provides a platform for this community online. The app allows one user to connect with and help another instantly from nearby or at any distance.

Sober Grid users can find other sober people nearby on The Grid— a GPS locator user interface that displays user profiles and distances from them. Users can also choose to remain anonymous. Sober Grid users can find sober friends while traveling, in an airport, or in a new city. Users can also enter the name of another user and locate them by geographic location to help find sober friends in other cities.

Users can log in to find sober people wherever they are. Sober Grid chat and messaging functions can be used by selecting individual profiles on The Grid. Sober Grid even has a feature that allows users to send their location to another user if they would like to meet up. Sober Grid's geo-social networking features help users find and connect with sober people locally and anywhere in the world.

Just like other popular social networks, Sober Grid users have access to our global newsfeed where they can communicate and share posts with other sober people.

Sober Grid is a safe place to share everyday thoughts, experiences and struggles associated with sobriety and addiction recovery.

Access to peer support is essential to continued sobriety and there are always users online to interact with and communicate to.[116]

But there is absolutely nothing safe and supportive about a user's data being appropriated by a third party corporation for profit, and there is absolutely nothing safe and supportive about sitting in solitude connecting with a complete stranger over a chain of privatized digital networks about matters of the utmost intimacy and vulnerability. When Sober Grid says that their platform is a "safe place" to share "everyday thoughts and experiences," what they are really saying is that "the world itself has become so barren and unsafe to share such matters, so might as well come here to our app instead." This is a case of where the presented cure is part of the very poison itself.

One of the principal investors of Sober Grid was former Massachusetts Governor and Vice Presidential candidate for the Libertarian Party Bill Weld. At a public event celebrating the initial launch of Sober Grid, Weld was asked what prompted him to invest in such a company and he responded, "We can do well while doing good."

What is interesting about Weld's response is how we can see a historical link between the core of the Puritanical New England *ethos*[117] — a lineage of which Weld is actually a direct descendent — and the emergent *ethos* of "conscious capitalism" in the age of 21st century neoliberal globalization. Both *ethos* rest upon the erection of an ideological screen so that a kind of symmetry can appear between unrestrained capitalist expansion and social benevolence.

Weld's comments — "We can do well while doing good" — appear almost humanitarian even as they are coming from a contemporary venture capitalist, almost in the exact same way the founding fathers of Lowell, Massachusetts — the prototypical "factory town" of 19th century American capitalism — spoke about the reasons for the construction of their utopian, industrialized project.[118] So Weld's comments not only disclose something about the disavowed pathological character of neoliberalism, but also how the very idea of recovery is in the process of a profound transformation in which its public and spiritual roots are being lost for a privatized and materialist replacement. From Weld's perspective, there is no real conflict in "doing good" and "doing well" — one can equally help society and maximize profit at the very same time, so there is no real conflict to these two basic human drives.

But there is a conflict today, *in the context of how Weld means it.* What we are seeing today in the linkage of globalized capitalism and computational technologies is the emergence of a global grid of exchange that is revealing itself to be progressively more rapacious, violent, and schizophrenic with every passing day. The abstract violence of capitalism is simply everywhere now:

Capitalism is what is left when beliefs have collapsed at the level of ritual or symbolic elaboration, and all that is left is the consumer-spectator, trudging through the ruins and the relics.[119]

One cannot help but note a profound disjuncture between the business model of Sober Grid and the spiritual core of a program such as Alcoholics Anonymous. Where Sober Grid is fundamentally predicated upon the potential to monetize the collective experience of recovery while aggregating data from its individual users, such behavior is expressly forbidden in the very by laws of Alcoholics Anonymous:

Alcoholics Anonymous will never have a professional class. We have gained some understanding of the ancient words "Freely ye

have received, freely give." We have discovered that at the point of professionalism, money and spirituality do not mix. Almost no recovery from alcoholism has ever been brought about by the world's best professionals, whether medical or religious. We do not decry professionalism in other fields, but we accept the sober fact that it does not work with us. Every time we have tried to professionalize our Twelfth Step[120], the result has been exactly the same: Our single purpose has been defeated.[121]

The underlying meaning of the above passage is that there must *necessarily* be a gap between the drive of capitalism and the drive of recovery. The neoliberal praxis that is now starting to define the experience of recovery from heroin addiction — equally seen in the explosion of pharmacological interventions and the emergence of platform recovery communities such as Sober Grid — is quite literally the opposite of the above passage: *they are purely professional*, they are purely mediated by capitalist mediation and technological efficiency, and therefore *de facto* are constitutionally absent the authentic feeling of charity and humanity. But this is the precise paradox of the neoliberal healing model: the central reason why so many have become heroin addicts in 21st century American society in the first place is because of the fact that they lived in a home, a community, and a world that was progressively stripped of these very feelings, sentiments, and memories that are now barred from neoliberal space.

We should be clear here and be certain that we are not throwing out the baby with the bath water. We are by no means trying to make a claim that all scientific research on the material roots of something like opiod addiction should be abandoned because they are "professional" and therefore contradict the "spiritual" principals of something like Alcoholics Anonymous. What we are rather saying is that when you are encountering something like the contemporary heroin crisis — a crisis that is fundamentally linked to the radical instrumentalization and individualization of global society — and approach it through the ideological frame of neoliberalism, you are essentially attempting to cure the disease with more of the very poison itself.

In an age where it is all too easy to look back and critique a program such as AA for its "naïve-ness" or its "lack of scientific data" to substantiate its healing claims, shouldn't we rather be focusing on the precious core of such a program: that it is a *public* program with no hidden financial motives other than to help another suffering member of society; that it is an anonymous, yet fully transparent fellowship with no desires to collect data on its members for the purpose of monetization or advertising (perhaps the deeper spiritual point of the principal of anonymity); and that its entire organizational structure is based upon an open system of checks, balances, and power sharing mechanisms between members — a wonderful example of true democracy in action.

But perhaps the ultimate lesson from a program such as Alcoholics Anonymous is that it discloses in no uncertain terms what is absolutely essential if there is ever to be a collective healing of this epidemic: which is the necessity to make such a moment an act of public will; a mobilization of bodies that are willing to encounter each other in the flesh and share their experience without any technical or corporate mediation.

But how is this even possible today when the entire social body has been effectively subsumed under a web of networks mediated by a pure capitalist logic, the logic of neoliberal globalization *par excellence*? What has happened to "the People" amidst this dynamic that perpetually atomizes and reduces society into either the most toxic forms of narcissistic individuality or mob behavior, minus any individualized consciousness and genuine solidarity:

The masses are actually fading, almost vanishing. The emergence of the post-mass media technology for networked communication has dispelled the crowd, turning it into a sprawl of connecting atoms, while the precarization of labor disintegrates the physical proximity of workers. Social precarity can, indeed, be described as a condition in which workers are continuously changing their individual positions so that nobody will ever meet anybody in the same place twice.[122]

Neurological Interventions

If the present heroin epidemic — an epidemic that is interestingly enough *not* swept under the proverbial rug by social authority, but rather routinely discoursed by politicians at all levels across the country — is ever to recede from the public sphere, we must not only confront the explicit violence of drug addiction itself, but also the structural and ideological conditions that have laid the groundwork for this epidemic to multiply so freely throughout the contemporary social landscape.

We can see this inability to directly encounter the socio-spiritual core of heroin addiction most clearly in the ongoing transformation of addiction management and recovery away from its public, non-profit dimension and into an entrepreneurial business model that is increasingly directed towards individual addicts; more specifically, the *individual brains* of addicts.[123] Meaning, the emergent model of drug rehabilitation along with the now prevalent public discourse circumscribing heroin addiction equally fails to see this epidemic as a *public crisis*; as a lucid indication of a spiraling collective pathology with profound long term effects yet to be realized. Instead, the causation of addiction is more and more displaced onto that of the individual addict him or herself which then in turn calls for individualized cure: this is the very "privatization" of drug rehabilitation that directly mirrors its underlying cause.

A clear demonstration of such a dramatic shift in our collective sensibilities can be located in the following piece regarding the ongoing research of an experimental compound known as PZM21, a compound that could eventually lead to a whole new class of opiates that would bind differently to the opiod receptors in the brain, thus being potentially less addictive than street heroin and the various other opiate based pharmaceuticals currently on the market.

What is perhaps most interesting about the following passage is how addiction is framed in such mechanical, nearly mathematic language:

addiction is not a devastating spiritual experience, it is not a problem of language, in that the experience of addiction evades all attempts to be properly symbolized into a chain of meaning, nor is it a problem of community, a problem of the intersubjective realm. No, heroin addiction is simply a problem of the opiate receptors in the human brain:

Each of these compounds binds to opioid receptors — specific proteins found in the brain, spinal cord and other organs in the body — just like morphine. But they activate a different signaling pathway, a route through which information flows from one molecule to another, than conventional opioids.

These distinctions mean the new opioids could decrease the risk of addiction and eliminate a leading cause of overdose death: respiratory depression. The fatal side effect drew attention recently after it was deemed the cause of death for popular pop artist Prince.

Brian Shoichet, professor of pharmaceutical chemistry at University of California, San Francisco, and co-author of a paper on PZM21 published last month in Nature, says eliminating this side effect is one of the most important goals in creating new opioids ...

Researchers are hoping new work in the field of opioid development can solve the problems caused by traditional opioids rather than treating the side effects and repair the reputation of opioids.

"I hope we can recognize this is a new way to approach treating this receptor," said Laura Bohn, a professor at Scripps Research Institute, who has studied opioid receptors for more than a decade. "And it comes at a time when the receptors are becoming very demonized in the media and politically."[124]

It is worth noting again that the principal concern of the researcher is "the opiate receptors" in the brain versus the actual suffering of the addict: "the receptors are becoming very demonized in the media and politically." In other words, the true victim here is *not* the addict, it is the opiod receptors in the brain. The logic here is that you don't treat the experience of the human being *as such*, you don't treat the authentic Other; rather, you reduce the addict's experience into a schema that can be addressed through a formal logic: in this case, a specific pharmaceutical intervention into the neuronal topography of the brain itself.

But such a statement of seeming scientific neutrality is not really a surprise in the least today, since it fits in perfectly with the basic logic of globalized Capital in the 21st century.

We are now rapidly moving into a world where capitalism itself is transforming before our eyes, where the logic of *pre-emption* is now to fashion in a deterministic way the future reality of the human subject. But this, as in the above case of PZM21, is not simply a purely "scientific" methodology to arrest the ongoing crisis of heroin addiction; it is also part of a broader ideological transformation of our very social substance within the era of neoliberal globalization: every neuron is to be accounted for in the future as the core logic of capitalism becomes the all-encompassing mediator of our experience.

The emergent model of addressing heroin addiction in contemporary American society — whether it be through group therapy sessions run by a for profit start-up, digital platforms that promise a new kind of recovery community, or the various pharmaceutical interventions into cerebral space — are all becoming increasingly *totalitarian,* all becoming increasingly rapacious in their desire to *monetize, quantify, and control* the experience of the addict.

Heroin as Ideology

Beyond the fiction of reality, there is the reality of the fiction.[125]

— *Slavoj Zizek*

It is always a highly problematic statement when the American politician of today says, something to the effect, "We are going to eradicate this opiate crisis once and for all." To make such a bold statement in 2018 is similar to saying, "We are going to eradicate the air you breathe once and for all." The countless American politicians throughout the country who have made the issue of heroin addiction a signature feature of their campaign or political platform — and therefore *de facto* required to make such a blanket statement — do not sufficiently realize, or perhaps does not want to realize, that opiate addiction has become integrated into the very fabric of 21st century American life. You can't "get rid of it" for the same reason that you can't "get rid of" Reality Television, Twitter feeds, and new mergers between multinational corporations: a socialized pathology like heroin addiction is actualized by the very same forces that structure our day to day lives; the very life experiences that we now view as neutral and non-pathological.

This is why the contemporary opiate epidemic should be characterized, not as an "ideological addiction," but rather as a specific type of addiction that bears witness to the presence of ideology in operation.

We should always remember that ideology, contrary to popular belief, is not simply that of a discernible fidelity to some clearly stated political or axiomatic belief structure, as in an allegiance to Soviet Communism, the Green movement, or Jehovah's Witness. The most powerful ideology, as Slavoj Zizek has reminded us all time and again, is in many ways the exact opposite. The most powerful ideology is operative when any system becomes so dominant, so part of our daily experience, that over time it eventually fades to the background and becomes naturalized; assumes an air of neutrality in which it ceases to appear positively or negatively charged. That is to say, ideology operates most effectively when we don't even realize we are within it and acting it out.

One of the (many) ways we can see ideology in action is in the multiple consumer products that now market themselves as being absent their negative properties:

On today's market, we find a whole series of products deprived of their malignant property: coffee without caffeine, cream without fat, beer without alcohol ... And the list goes on: what about virtual sex as sex without sex, the Colin

Powell doctrine of warfare with no casualties (on our side, of course) as warfare without warfare, the contemporary redefinition of politics as the art of expert administration as politics without politics, up to today's tolerant liberal multiculturalism as an experience of Other deprived of its Otherness ... ? Virtual Reality simply generalizes this procedure of offering a product deprived of its substance: it provides reality itself deprived of its substance - in the same way decaffeinated coffee smells and tastes like the real coffee without being the real one, Virtual Reality is experienced as reality without being one. Is this not the attitude of today's hedonistic Last Man? Everything is permitted, you can enjoy everything, BUT deprived of its substance which makes it dangerous.[126]

On October 26, 2017 President Trump — surrounded by both top government officials and families from around the country who have tragically lost loved ones to heroin addiction — gave a policy speech at the White House in which he outlined his strategy to combat the opiate crisis. We should read Trump's following remarks about the heroin epidemic against this very background elucidated in the above passage:

As you all know from personal experience, families, communities, and citizens across our country are currently dealing with the worst drug crisis in American history and even, if

you really think about it, world history. This is all throughout the world. The fact is this is a worldwide problem.

This crisis of drug use, addiction, and overdose deaths in many years, it's just been so long in the making. Addressing it will require all of our effort and it will require us to confront the crisis in all of its very real complexity.

Last year, we lost at least 64,000 Americans to overdoses. That's 175 lost American lives per day. That's seven lost lives per hour in our country. Drug overdoses are now the leading cause of unintentional death in the United States by far ...

At my direction, the National Institute of Health, headed up by Francis Collins, has taken the first steps of an ambitious public-private partnership with pharmaceutical companies to develop non-addictive painkillers and new treatments for addiction and overdose. So important.

I will be pushing the concept of non-addictive painkillers very, very hard. We have to come up with that solution. We give away billions and billions of dollars a year, and we're going to be spending lots of money on coming up with a non-addictive solution.

We will be asking Dr. Collins and the NIH for substantial resources in the fight against drug addiction. One of the things our administration will be doing is a massive advertising campaign to get people, especially children, not to

want to take drugs in the first place because they will see the devastation and the ruination it causes to people and people's lives.

Watch what happens, if we do our jobs, how the number of drug users and the addicted will start to tumble downward over a period of years. It will be a beautiful thing to see.[127]

What is this "non-addictive painkiller" that Trump refers to in his speech? Is this not perhaps the ultimate example of trying to gloss over, to disavow, to ideologically mitigate the inherent problem of opiates: what makes a class of drugs like opiates so problematic *is* the very fact that they are addictive. There is simply no such thing as a "non-addictive" opiate in the same way that there is no such thing as a pork chop absent the meat of a pig. When you take away this feature from an opiate — the very feature that brings forth its explosive potential as both an individual and social pathology — it ceases even to be an opiate as such.

So when President Trump gives a policy speech about the haunting specter of opiate addiction in American society — and then regresses into ridiculous solutions such as "non-addictive painkillers" and "a massive advertising campaign" — it bears further witness to the fact that what the crisis of opiate addiction signifies in contemporary American society is not only something profound but something inherently traumatic; something that we do not want to fully account for. And this is precisely why the presence of heroin addiction throughout 21st century American society — from the redwood forest to the gulf stream waters — calls for ideological mediation.

It is almost incredible to realize that the famous quip from Marx that "religion is the opium of the people," is becoming literally actualized today in 21st century America: *opium is the opium of the people*:

Religion is the sigh of the oppressed creature, the heart of a heartless world, and the soul of soulless conditions. It is the opium of the people. The abolition of religion as the illusory happiness of the people is the demand for their real happiness. To call on them to give up their illusions about their condition is to call on them to give up a condition that requires illusions. The criticism of religion is, therefore, in embryo, the criticism of that vale of tears of which religion is the halo.[128]

The point Marx makes here is that the critique of ideology is only the critique of "an illusion," that which blocks the potential to encounter the world as it is and actualize "real happiness." It is a similar thing here with heroin addiction in the present: is not the descent into the heroin crisis simply "the sigh of the oppressed creature," a signifier of the collective "soul of a soulless condition." To collectively sober up from the heroin crisis requires the culture to lose the very illusion that underlies the escape into heroin in the first place.

The heroin addict of the present symbolically functions as the "zombie" of globalized capitalism: not because they are inherently monstrous people, but rather because they have been progressively de-subjectified by the various processes of neoliberal globalization. In a different way you could say that the heroin addict is the excess of the system, *but within the boundaries of the system itself.*

There is a similarity here between the heroin addict and the refugee from the various devastated Third World zones of the global south. The refugee can also be characterized as the excess of the contemporary global order. But the refugee, by definition, exists on the periphery of the system whereas the heroin addict is *immanent* to the topography of global capitalism itself: regarded almost as the proverbial trash that cannot effectively be brought out to the garbage.

So what is ideological here is the fact that there is no direct link in framing this crisis between the rise of neoliberalism and the rise of the heroin addict as a contemporary subjectivity: such a link, when it is even seen, is seen as a purely contingent phenomenon. What happens instead is that the heroin addict simply appears as an unfortunate, but "naturalized" feature of life in 21st century America. It is a case of, "Yes, of course it's sad, but that's just how it is today." *How what is today?* is the question that should be immediately posed against such a statement. Is this scenario, a country full of heroin junkies, "just the way things are, just the way the world works?" The uncomfortable truth is that if you really listen to many of our politicians, or the discourses of the pharmaceutical industrial complex, this is precisely what they are essentially saying: it's sad, but that's just how it goes today.

How what goes?

The ideology of global capitalism insists on treating the heroin epidemic as if it were a fact of the universe, like the sun rising in the east every morning. And this "naturalization" of the heroin crisis, which then is handed over to various scientific discourses so to debate about potential solutions and medical interventions, disavows any political causation: this is the very definition of an ideological operation, just the way Althusser himself would say it:

… ideology 'acts' or 'functions' in such a way that it 'recruits' subjects among the individuals (it recruits them all), or 'transforms' the individuals into subjects (it transforms them all) by that very precise operation that we call interpellation or hailing, and which can be imagined along the lines of the most commonplace everyday police (or other) hailing: 'Hey, you there!'[129]

This is Althussser's famous analogy, that an ideological operation is like a cop yelling at a passing pedestrian: "Hey, you there!" The point is not that the pedestrian immediately stops because he senses his guilt for some undiscovered crime, the point is that even if the pedestrian is a saint, she will necessarily question her own innocence and thus naturally respond to the call: ideology "calls us" to respond to life in a certain way. And this is exactly how we are collectively responding to the heroin crisis, we are being "called" to respond in a certain way, being "called" to see this crisis from a certain perspective that disavows any socioeconomic causation; reducing addiction to a purely that of a neuronal or genetic pathology.

And this is why so many politicians' hands are ultimately tied on this issue, even as they continue to make bold claims about arresting its proliferation throughout American society; perfectly exemplified in the above comments of President Trump. And their hands are tied because if they were to actually link neoliberalism with heroin addiction, their whole world view, their whole view of the global economy that makes perfectly logical sense to them, would essentially disintegrate before their eyes.

Just Say No!

In 1604 King James I, when taking account of the surge of tobacco use amongst the British population after the plant was imported by the early planters of Virginia, penned a royal decree condemning this novel practice that had suddenly infiltrated English society:

> **And now good Country man, let us (I pray you) consider what honor or policie can move us to imitate the slavish Indians, especially in so vile and stinking custom ... I say without blushing, (why do we) abase ourselves so farre, as to imitate these beastly Indians, slaves to the Spaniards and refuse to the world, and yet as aliens to the Holy Covenant of God? Why do we not as well imitate them in walking naked as they doe? ... Yes, why do we not denie God and adore the Devil, as they doe?[130]**

Is this not the supreme model of what Power does with the very problems that it itself creates? The British crown and its surrounding aristocracy — those same people that bankrolled the rape and pillage of the entire world in their never ending obsession for profit and power from the trade in tea, spices, and opium; those same people that were chiefly responsible for exporting slavery to the southern American colonies — are now playing the role of the defender of morality and decency when the very same socioeconomic forces they unleash re-materialize in their own backyard? This is precisely the point that the American civil rights leader Malcolm X once made — and it is a point that is both theoretically sophisticated as well as containing profound common sense — when he said, "the chickens have come home to roost."

Jacques Lacan made a similar point in his famous quip, *The letter always arrives at its destination.* With the contemporary heroin crisis, is this not a clear case of, "the letter arriving at its destination?": the letter (the heroin epidemic itself) arriving at its destination (a socially fragmented, psychologically and emotionally traumatized population).

The scenario that frustrated King James I now plays itself out again, in yet another guise, with the rise of the modern opiate crisis. The initial surge of illegal OxyContin addiction that followed the drug's release onto the market in 1996 was directly aided and abetted by the FDA and their links to the pharmaceutical industrial complex, the very same governmental agency that had the duty to protect Americans from such a possibility. Soon after the drug's release, as aptly chronicled by journalist Beth Macey in her 2018 expose *Dopesick*, alarm bells were being sounded loud and clear in different locations throughout America, particularly the Appalachia region of West Virginia and eastern Kentucky:

Despite all the technical, medical, and political sophisti-cation developed over the past century, despite the regula-tory initiatives and the so-called War on Drugs, few people batted an eye in the late 1990s as a new wave of opiod addiction crept onto the prescription pads of America's doctors ...[131]

And even when there were early attempts to incite some kind of political mobilization and public awareness about this gestating crisis, such attempts were all effectively squashed by the lobbying power and "confirmed science" of Purdue Pharma. Their product, an incredibly addictive painkiller that was in process of becoming a full blown public health crisis, was given ideological cover by framing it as an essential pharmaceutical product for people around the country that were suffering from legitimate pain; and that its entrance onto the illegal market was simply a glitch, an unfortunate side effect that bore no relevance to the essential nature of the product itself.

But ten years later, after the social devastation became too great to bear and there was finally some political will mobilized to put some restrictions on Oxycontin, it was effectively too late: these powerful opiates had infiltrated the collective brain of 21st century American society and the turn to heroin was effectively made:

Sam Quiones, the author of *Dreamland*, encapsulates the shift from Oxycontin to heroin in the following passage:

By the end of the 2000's it was already common for people to go from abusing Oxycontin to a heroin habit. Purdue Pharma recognized this and in 2010 reformulated Oxycontin with an abuse deterrent, making the drug harder to deconstruct and inject. The intent was to make Oxy less abusable. It did. Had the company done this in 1996, our story may have been different. But now there was a swollen population of Oxy addicts nationwide. Without Oxy, they flocked to heroin in even greater numbers.

Fast food restaurants developed a heroin problem. Across the country, people were using their convenience bathrooms as places to shoot up. There, locked in isolation, many overdosed and died. In Boston, the problem got so bad that the city's public health commission asked fast food workers to do periodic bathroom checks, and began training workers to notice the signs of an overdose: a person's slowed breathing, or lips turning blue.

Alabama now had heroin. Mississippi and southern Louisiana did, too. Rural towns in Indiana and Oregon were bad. Eastern Idaho, North Dakota, and Wyoming were, too.[132]

What we have, first and foremost, with the American heroin epidemic is a crisis of bodies, a crisis of neuronal connections, a crisis of the flesh: we can never overlook that material and biological fact as to where this crisis ultimately metastasizes. And then, supplementing that materiality, what we also have is a cultural crisis, a public crisis, and a crisis of community.

But what we also have, and what is often most overlooked about the heroin epidemic, is the fact this also signifies an ideological crisis.

What is ideological is not so much the fact that the combination of lax FDA approval mechanisms and the corporate lobbying power of companies like Purdue Pharma eventually helped to spawn the national heroin crisis that is now being addressed by even the The President of the United States. What is truly "ideological" here — that is to say, what is *invisible,* what covers the gaps and inconsistencies in the field of meaning — is the fact that heroin addiction is used to obfuscate the very crisis that has produced *itself*: the crisis of neoliberalism, the crisis of globalized capitalism, the crisis of networked technologies.

In other words, heroin is representative of both a sickness and an attempt to cure the very sickness at the same time. It is a way to avoid truly encountering the extent of the political and cultural devastation that is now occurring all around us.

What this means is that heroin addiction is not necessarily the problem itself, but rather a strategy used by a whole generation of addicts around the country to avoid really seeing what the problem is.

The Search for Meaning

Things change everyday, Mr. Nakata. With each new dawn, it's not

the same world as the day before. And you're not the same person as you

were, either. You get what I'm saying? Connections change too. Who's

the capitalist, who's the proletarian. Who's on the right, who's on the left.

The information revolution, stock options, floating assets, occupational

restructuring, multinational corporations — what's good, what's bad.

Boundaries between things are changing all the time. Maybe that's why

you can't speak to cats anymore.[133]

— *Haruki Murakami, Kafka on the Shore*

Allow me to now speak as a former addict, as a person who for nearly three years was hopelessly addicted to both Oxycontin and heroin, as a person who has injected this drug into his veins and knows full well the problem of heroin:

I am able to speak directly to this experience.

I feel there are three basic categories of drug users. This armchair classification system is generated only from what I myself have perceived and experienced throughout my life. I call the first category "the social group." The second I call "the dope group." And the third I call "the psychedelic group." And of course, it goes without saying that there are countless variations and permutations between these three primary categories; they are by no means mutually exclusive.

The first grouping, whose principal drugs of choice are alcohol and cocaine, at least in the beginning, tend to be more extraverted and more social. Their gravitation towards drinking alcohol and using a drug like cocaine tends to coincide with a particular social constellation in which they *want* to be part of — like being in high school and wanting to drink with the football team, a ridiculously clichéd but symbolically valid example of the American high school experience. Constitutive of the first group is the presence of certain competitive pressures that are externalized into the social field, in which alcohol consumption and a drug like cocaine can act as a crutch of sorts, as a mode of existential support, so the person can feel to be participating more fully in their social network.

The second grouping, which would be inclusive of the personality that would eventually gravitate towards heroin addiction, tends to be more introspective, and more isolated from their own personal network of friends and family. The second group is also far less interested in keeping up the façade of appearances that in many ways defines the early stages of the first group before addiction sets in. These people are usually at least partially conscious that they are starved of their own feelings, *of their own experience,* and have an interest in a substance or process that will allow them to enter into a dialogue with themselves rather than the Other. A drug like heroin, in the beginning, is able to materialize this experience and interior dialogue for the user.

The third group tends to be far more interested in the questions and issues that could be characterized as "transpersonal." Whereas the first group has interest in interacting with the Other, the second in interacting with Oneself, the third has an interest in having a dialogue with the various structures and systems that mediate our collective experience. Questions of ecology, questions as to the validity of the various economic and social forms that define humanity, and of course, questions of consciousness and of God.

The first time I ever tried Oxycontin was in the spring of 2001 while I was in college when I was home in Boston visiting family and friends for a weekend. The event didn't strike me as anything unusual at the time, as if I was even remotely conscious of the explosive potential for this drug to catalyze soon after into a nationwide epidemic that would eventually mutate into the heroin crisis of today. At the time it rather seemed to be that of a one-off moment, an irreverent instance of experimentation with a new drug that simply happened to be in the same room as I was. It was explained to me as simply a "strong painkiller," which sounded fine at the time, nor did it ring any immediate alarm bells.

What I remember most from that night was how tired it made me. I can still see myself that night, as if playing back an old video in my mind that I am watching from an exteriorized position, sitting on a green leather couch aimlessly watching television, effectively unable to move or speak. I had experimented with other painkillers before that night, such as Percocet and Vicodin, but none of these other pharmaceuticals had remotely the power that I was experiencing this evening. But, and even with the intense high, it was not as if I became addicted the next morning, as if I bought a supply that I could bring back with me to my college campus. I simply chalked it up as a strong pill, but I didn't give it much thought for the time being.

Addiction is a strange thing, a peculiar phenomenon. And it is most peculiar in how it metastasizes itself in a person's experience: for some addiction comes on strong and hard, it produces an immediate and insatiable craving where one senses the specter of addiction from the very beginning. For others it creeps up silently before eventually revealing itself in all of its power. And this latter experience was that of my own: I did not realize I was addicted until I fully realized I was in fact an addict. And that realization, the authentic recognition that your own agency has been foreclosed by a foreign substance, is an absolutely horrifying revelation.

Far before my own cognition regarding the fact of my personal addiction — but very soon after my initial encounter with Oxycontin — I began to hear multiple stories about people I had known in and around the greater Boston area getting hooked on Oxycontin; even resorting to stealing to keep up the habit. And this was not just abstract knowledge, such as stories in the newspaper, because I personally knew these people.

But still, even with the seriousness of the situation becoming more and more evident, nothing dawned on me yet. That is to say, there was nothing indicating to me that this obscure pharmaceutical drug was going to so deeply effect the entire country and eventually open the door to the 21st century heroin crisis, or that I was going to become an addict myself, or that I would eventually write a book on the subject. There was simply no way to properly theoretically gauge what I was then observing, there was no way to put this burgeoning local crisis into a universal chain of meaning.

We have mentioned that when a drug appears in a culture as an essentialized fact of life —— as in, "Everyone is doing heroin these days" — although such a statement speaks to a pure contingency, there is something essential *about* the contingency in question. Of course, there is nothing essential about heroin use in the greater Boston area. As far as I know the original Puritans weren't using heroin or pharmaceutical grade opiods when they arrived in 1630 on the *Arabella*. Nor did the wave of Irish Catholic migrants that began to arrive in the 1840s that would forever transform this city's cultural and political fabric have any association with opiate addiction. But there was absolutely something essential about this contingent moment in Boston's unfolding history, the very moment when the city would undergo a devastating addiction crisis just at the time it would fully encounter a globalized world at the dawn of the 21st century.

In my book *There is No Such Thing as Boston: Gentrification and the Disappearance of a City* I spoke about the seemingly strange coincidence between the surge of gentrification (which is simply neoliberal globalization applied to the urban topography) and the surge of Oxycontin and heroin addiction that suddenly infected the various working class neighborhoods that had once constituted the majority of Boston's population at the precise same time. As the surge of young, cognitive professionals — social agents completely disconnected from any and all local neighborhood networks or particular ethnicities with historical ties in the city of Boston — began to take over Boston's residential population, the remaining working class residents — those with historical and familial ties into their particular neighborhood where they resided — experienced what can only be called a collective crisis of both opiate addiction and gentrification:

In this very sense, the interrelationship between the double surge of gentrification on one hand, and Oxycontin on the other, in Boston neighborhoods at the turn of the century points to something even more fundamental: they are both symptomatic of a global economy dramatically transforming: production completely dislodging itself from time and place and beginning to operate in the virtual, financial, and global spheres.[134]

There can be no doubt that there is a direct link between Oxycontin and heroin, there can be no doubt that the genealogy tracing 21st century opiate addiction begins with the epidemic of Oxycontin abuse in the 2000s that then morphed into the heroin crisis of the 2010s. But, it seems that the expert class who have thus far commented on the opiate crisis have made this correlation entirely based on Oxycontin's particular chemical composition: that is to say, the relationship between this pharmaceutical product's concentrated potency of opiods and the social consequences of addiction. The thinking goes that perhaps if Oxycontin was structured more like Percocet or Vicodin —- opiate based pharmaceuticals with far less concentrated opiod content — then the heroin epidemic could have been avoided in the first place. This reading of the opiate crisis should be rejected. And the reason it should be rejected is because such a commentary completely disavows the real forces that were ultimately responsible for the opiate epidemic to spread throughout 21st century American culture.

In other words, there was ultimately far less differentiation between Oxycontin and other opiate based pharmaceuticals on the market than the expert class has claimed; it wasn't Oxycontin itself that was necessarily so different, but rather *the times* that we were living in that were truly different. This seemingly "scientific" position — "if only Oxycontin was released onto the market with an opiod concentration of x instead of y ..." — is actually the true pie in the sky, idealistic position. The uncomfortable fact of the matter is that American culture was in many ways already addicted to Oxycontin *before* it even came onto the market; the introduction of Oxycontin onto the market simply confirmed the fact. This is by no means giving a free pass to a corporation like Purdue Pharma and their incredibly irresponsible decision to release and market to the unsuspecting public such a profoundly dangerous drug. They were wrong and they always will be wrong for their unconscionable actions. But, nevertheless, the chain of socialized trauma that seems to have been initiated by

Oxycontin had far less to do with its particular chemical structure than the society who became so easily addicted to it.

The Lacanian interpretation of trauma could be helpful here to assist in making our point.[135] For Lacan trauma is that of a shattering of the coordinates that grounds a person's (or in our case a culture's) symbolic identity. Experiencing a violent assault, losing a loved one, being forced to experience some kind of political upheaval — the potential list of traumatic events goes on indefinitely. Trauma ultimately bears witness to a symbolic disintegration, an event that signifies that "things are simply no longer the same:" when things can never go back to the way they were before the traumatic event entered into our life and forever altered it. But things get very interesting here as the Lacanian theory further develops, that the event when the traumatic impact seems to have occurred is actually not the trauma itself. Rather, the impact of the traumatic intrusion rather bears witness to the fact that the trauma *has already occurred, that it has already taken place.* For Lacan, counter-intuitively, what we usually think of as trauma is actually the very thing that helps us *make sense of what has already happened.*

This is what I meant by saying, "American culture was in many ways already addicted to Oxycontin before it came onto the market: the introduction of Oxycontin onto the market simply confirmed the fact." What this means is that it is a mistake to claim that the epidemic of Oxycontin and heroin, *in itself,* signifies a point blank traumatic event to American culture; that this crisis is simply indicative of corrupted pharmaceutical companies and corrupted South American cartels traumatizing America's youth for profit. Although this is of course true from a certain perspective, the deeper truth is that America's youth were *already* profoundly traumatized, they had *already* lost their symbolic grounding: the entrance of Oxycontin actually served as a way to give this collective trauma a sense of *meaning*.[136] To put it another way, the true trauma isn't getting hit with shrapnel on a remote battlefield in Iraq; the real trauma is getting on the military plane to go there and fight in the first place: the shrapnel simply confirms the fact that trauma has in fact already occurred.

But something like trauma, no matter in what shape or form it enters into our life, no matter how devastating or painful it may be, it necessarily opens up a space by which healing can occur, where the sense of wholeness can return in a new way: trauma is actually a way to go to back to the beginning, *again*. If the definition of trauma is that of a symbolic disintegration, then by definition it must also entail the potential to reshape those very same symbolic coordinates that have thus been eroded. In this sense, trauma is a gift that opens the possibility for a new horizon of meaning to open.

In Haruki Murakami's novel *Kafka on the Shore*, he provides what I feel to be one of the truly great definitions of the traumatic experience in contemporary literature:

And you really will have to make it through that violent, metaphysical, symbolic storm. No matter how metaphysical or symbolic it might be, make no mistake about it: it will cut through flesh like a thousand razor blades. People will bleed

there, and you will bleed too. Hot, red blood. You'll catch that blood in your hands, your own blood and the blood of others.

And once the storm is over you won't remember how you made it through, how you managed to survive. You won't even be sure, in fact, whether the storm is really over. But one thing is certain. When you come out of the storm you won't be the same person who walked in. That's what this storm's all about.[137]

The key line here is the fact that you won't be the same person, *literally*: if you take the opening that the traumatic intrusion offers to its outer limit, you will come through the experience as a new person. And what is different, what has changed, is a person's own symbolic identification: trauma is the great purifier of life, in that it reduces our psychic and spiritual apparatus to its bare necessity, which is the very place where true and profound symbolic regeneration can occur.

We have thus far been speaking about the heroin addict and his or her capacity to heal from addiction, which is the task of re-symbolizing one's identity to open up a new field of meaning. And in many ways, this is also the great task that the world must undertake in order to effectively respond to the incredible chaos and continual evisceration of meaning that is now being caused by the emergent forces of cognitive automation, Artificial Intelligence, and a fully operational globalized capitalism. Meaning is something that always minimally registers in the future, it is the way in which we gauge our passage through time and space. But the future is now disappearing, it is collapsing under the pressures of digital real time and the instrumentalization of every nook and cranny of human life.

American Dreaming

The "American Dream" was always a way to articulate something indelible about the American experience and spirit: self-sufficiency, the idea that responsibility and freedom go hand in hand, and the notion that progress is a rising tide. Of course, the content of this collective dream took different shapes and forms throughout history, but nevertheless, even in its historic multiplicity, a sense of universality persisted throughout the generations regarding this collective Dream. Even in the early 2000s, at the time I graduated from college, it seemed as if the generation I was part of still maintained a minimal belief in this American Dream; that we all still passively assumed we would naturally surpass our parents in living standards and quality of life, that we would find a stable long term job with continuous opportunities for upward mobility and professional growth.

The fact of the matter is that the America we were about to inherit would offer us no such guarantees that were afforded to the Greatest Generation, the Baby Boomers, or even Generation X.[138] Maybe in a way we were feigning in this belief of the system just to keep up appearances, maybe we knew all along that the gig was effectively up. Maybe in a way my generation's descent into a collective opiate addiction was paradoxically a mechanism to keep the very illusion of the American Dream alive. Meaning, rather than engaging in a direct questioning of the system we were about to inherit following the turn of the century, a system that was in its early stages of decay, we used opiates as our scapegoat, as a way not to experience that very symbolic death of this so called American Dream.

Zizek has spoken about this mechanism of displaced belief throughout his writings[139], how the loss of faith is most shattering not when we stop believing, but when we discover those we had thought believed all along never even did. I think a similar mechanism was at play here. Didn't we, the 21st century generation of opiate addicts and dope fiends, play the same game? By descending into the nightmare of addiction we were able to pretend that it was we alone who were sick, that it was we alone who were broken, versus facing the fact that it was the political, economic, and social fabric of our country that were making us all sick; that they were the ones that were *really* broken.

If there is a signature feature of 21st century globalized capitalism it is the colonization of meaning. That is to say, it is the fact that every single aspect of our lives is now subject to the law of profit, to the neo-liberal law of optimization, efficiency, and competition.[140] This may have always been the driving force of capitalism, just as Marx correctly noted in the 19th century. But what is different today is that this same pathological drive to turn all human value into pure instruments of equivalence and exchange has somehow evolved into something even more nefarious, more all encompassing. What is now different is the fact that capitalism has evolved to a point — with the incredible development of computational technologies, networks, and algorithmic intelligence — that such a drive can now be actualized in a much more direct and brutal way than it ever could have within the "analog world." To effectively describe the *modus operandi* of globalized capitalism today is to simply note that it has extended itself "beyond the confines of the factory or office building," and that it has extended itself "beyond the confines of the 9-5 shift." But not only has it colonized the entirety of our lived experience, far beyond simply our economic productivity, but it has become literally embedded within the functionality of our cells and neurons; it has infected our very souls.

The drive toward heroin addiction is thus the drive to find meaning in a world that is being systematically stripped of meaning in an *objective manner*. What we have here is an entirely different situation from when William Burroughs wrote *Junkie*, the 1950s addict as the individual eking out an existence in the dirty crevices and cracks outside the formal structures of the capitalist horizon. The heroin addict uses today precisely because there are no cracks or crevices even left, for the entirety of the world is being coded and quantified within a global network that no one can effectively escape.

The Beauty of Pockets

The British art critic John Berger invoked the idea of "the shape of a pocket" to describe potential zones of resistance to neoliberal capitalism. Berger begins by describing the general coordinates of the situation at hand: that we have now entirely moved beyond any and all past interpretations of the world horizon into what he terms as a "Fourth World War" — a dispersive and fragmented war run by global corporations against humanity:

The aim of the belligerents is the conquest of the entire world through the market. The arsenals are financial; there are nevertheless millions of people being killed or maimed every moment. The aim of those waging the war is to rule the world from new, abstract power centers — megapoles of the market, which will be subject to no control except that of the logic of investment. Meanwhile, nine-tenths of the women and men living on the planet live within the jagged pieces that do not fit ...[141]

Berger then goes on to describe a series of what he calls "pockets of resistance," the various peoples and groups around the world that are actively resisting the abstract and objective violence of global capitalism:

... The seventh piece of the puzzle has the shape of a pocket, and consists of all the pockets of resistance against the new order which are developing across the globe. The Zapatistas in south-east Mexico are one such pocket. Others, in different circumstances, have not necessarily chosen armed resistance. The many pockets do not have a common political program as such. How could they, existing as they do in the broken puzzle? Yet their heterogeneity may be a promise. What they have in common is their defense of the redundant, the next-to-be eliminated, and their belief that the Fourth World War is a crime against humanity.[142]

I would like to propose here that we extend Berger's list and definitively add the *global* recovery community as a potential pocket of resistance. They absolutely qualify as a group that has been devastated, definitively traumatized, by this "Fourth World War": the war being waged by global markets and global corporations against the people of Earth.

▲

It seems that we have now become too smart for our own good. We are rapidly developing technology to send a manned mission to Mars, to send tourists into outer space, to bring about previously undreamt of possibilities with the development of nanotechnologies, biotechnological interventions, and quantum computing — but yet we seem to have forgotten the sun rises in the east every morning. We are undoubtedly, as 21st century human beings, of the scientific vanguard. But spiritually, we are of a generation that is regressing the human race to a new Dark Age; we have lost both the notion of common sense and the notion of the People.

Although mentioning such a juxtaposition is by no means a new observation, in many ways Adorno and Horkheimer's *The Dialectic of Enlightenment* was predicated upon a similar critique. But we should say it again even louder today, for the new forms of totalitarianism that have emerged directly from the continuing application of "instrumental reason" in the present – Reality Television, Twitter feeds, a Big Data that makes Big Brother look like a very little brother – are in the process of creating an entire society of psychological and spiritual gulags; a seeming infinite archipelago of alienated and disconnected human beings robbed of their basic spiritual dignity, social interdependence, and economic responsibility.

The contemporary heroin addict is a symbol, he is a symbol that bears witness to this very socialized trauma. But, at the very same time, she is also a symbol of hope, of what could come after "wiping the slate clean" and opening to promise and potential of healing. And although it is absolutely essential for our culture to recover from opiate addiction, it is also essential to recover from the unconscionable trauma leveled against the basic dignity and freedom of human beings around the world over the past several decades, and to find new ways to revitalize the eternal human needs: friendship, community, local sensibility and culture, and basic respect for each other in the public spaces that define our worlds.

THE END

Notes

1. Saramago, J. (2003) *The cave*. New York: Harcourt. pg. 303-304

2. Han, B. (2017). *Psychopolitics: Neoliberalism and new technologies of power*. London: Verso. Kindle Edition.Kindle Edition. Location 48

3. Glatter, M. R. (2015, November 30). LSD Microdosing: The New Job Enhancer In Silicon Valley And Beyond. Retrieved from https://www.forbes.com/sites/robertglatter/2015/11/27/lsd-microdosing-the-new-job-enhancer-in-silicon-valley-and-beyond/#4380bfad188a

4. Somerville, H., May, P., & Bay Area News Group. (2014, July 29). Silicon Valley's killer app. Retrieved from https://www.mercurynews.com/2014/07/28/silicon-valleys-killer-app/

5. Lehman, P. (2018, February 12). Good news, bad news: Opioid prescriptions down in Pennsylvania, but ... Retrieved from http://www.mcall.com/news/breaking/mc-nws-opioid-prescriptions-20180109-story.html

6. Berardi, F. (2017). *Futurability: the age of impotence and the horizon of possibility.* Brooklyn: Verso Books. Kindle Edition. pgs. 49-56.

7. Fisher, M. (2010). *Capitalist realism: is there no alternative?* Winchester, UK: Zero Books. Kindle Edition. Location 332-340.

8. Ibid.

9. See for instance, "The Genetics of Addiction: Where Do We Go From Here" https://www.jsad.com/doi/full/10.15288/jsad.2016.77.673

10. This is not to idealize the industrial economy as the model we should be aspiring too. Nor it is to gloss over the racism and misogyny and homophobia that such a system produced. It is rather to contrast the function of fixed capital (factories, machines, etc.) and how such direct investment would naturally produce the sense of the future, versus the mobile, digital, 'real time,' mode of capital today.

11. Berardi, F., Genosko, G., & Thoburn, N. (2011). *After the future.* Edinburgh: AK Press. pgs. 23-25

12. Bauman, Z. (2017). A chronicle of crisis: 2011-2016. London: Social Europe Edition. Kindle Edition. pgs. 46-50

13. Han, B. (2015). *The burnout society.* Stanford, CA: Stanford Briefs. Kindle Edition. pg. 8

14. Ebert, J. D. (2013). *Art After Metaphysics.* Create Space. pgs. 121-122

15. Han, B. (2015). *The burnout society.* Stanford, CA: Stanford Briefs. Kindle Edition. pg. 19

16. Han, B. (2015) *The transparent society.* Stanford, CA: Stanford Press. Kindle Edition. See chapter 1, "The society of positivity."

17. Badiou, A., Gauchet, M., Duru, M., Legros, M., and Spitzer, S. (2016). *What is to be done?: a dialogue on communism, capitalism, and the future of democracy.* Cambridge: Polity. Kindle Edition. pgs. 64-66

18. Srnicek, N. (2017). *Platform capitalism.* Cambridge, UK: Polity. Kindle Edition. pgs. 88-92

19. "Time, Acceleration, and Violence." Retrieved from https://www.e-flux.com/journal/27/67999/time-acceleration-and-violence/

20. Friedman, T. (2016) *Thank you for being late.* New York: Farrar, Straus and Giroux. pg. 95

21. Berry, W. (2010). *What are people for?:10 essays.* Berkeley, CA: Counterpoint. Kindle Edition. pg. 135

22. Berry, W. (2016). *Our only world: ten essays.* Berkeley, CA: Counterpoint. Kindle Edition. pgs. 10-11. See chapter 1, "Paragraphs from a Notebook."

23. Han, B. (2015). *The burnout society.* Stanford, CA: Stanford Briefs. Kindle Edition. pg. 35-37

24. Ibid.

25. Han, B. (2015) *The transparent society.* Stanford, CA: Stanford Press. Kindle Edition. pg. 5, "On the one hand, they are giving way to enjoyment without negativity. On the other, their place has been taken by psychic disturbances such as exhaustion, fatigue, and depression—all of which are to be traced back to the excess of positivity."

26. See original Apple commercial, "Think Different," https://www.youtube.com/watch?v=cFEarBzelBs

27. Zizek, S. (2018) *Like a thief in broad daylight: power in the era of post humanity*. UK: Allen Lane. Kindle Edition. pgs. 4-5. Zizek says here, "Today's nihilism – the reign of cynical opportunism accompanied by permanent anxiety – legitimizes itself as the liberation from the old constraints: we are free to constantly re-invent our sexual identities, to change not only our job or our professional trajectory but even our innermost subjective features like our sexual orientation. However, the scope of these freedoms is strictly prescribed by the coordinates of the existing system, and also by the way consumerist freedom effectively functions: the possibility to choose and consume imperceptibly turns into a superego obligation to choose." Here he describes a key feature of the structural neoliberal terrain, in the sense that someone like Tony Robbins strangely functions as a super-ego agent, not preventing us from doing things, but getting us to fully identify with our desires that can be realized within a capitalist system.

28. Han, B. (2017). *Psychopolitics: Neoliberalism and new technologies of power*. London: Verso. Kindle Edition. See chapter 1, "The Crisis of Freedom."

29. Robbins, T. *Awaken the giant within: how to immediately take control mental, physical, emotional, and financial destiny*. (1992) New York: Simon and Schuster. pg. 164

30. Beradi, F. (2009) *The soul at work: from alienation to autonomy*. South Pasadena: Semiotexte. pgs. 74-77

31. See, https://www.e-flux.com/journal/27/67999/time-acceleration-and-violence/

32.   Han, B. (2015). *The burnout society*. Stanford, CA: Stanford Briefs. Kindle Edition. pg. 11-12

33.   Friedman, T. (2016) *Thank you for being late*. New York: Farrar, Straus and Giroux. pg. 219

34.   ibid.

35.   See, https://www.e-flux.com/announcements/124570/e-flux-journal-86-strange-universalism-guest-edited-by-hito-steyerl/

36.   Fisher, M. (2010). *Capitalist realism: is there no alternative?* Winchester, UK: Zero Books. Kindle Edition. pg. 4

37.   Wolny, P. (2014). *The truth about heroin*. New York: Rosen Publishing. pgs. 15-25

38.   ibid.

39.   ibid.

40.   Žižek, S. (2008). *In Defense of Lost Causes*. London: Verso. pg. 190

41.   ibid.

42.   See,https://economicsociology.org/2017/08/13/the-virtue-of-having-nothing-to-say/

43.   See, Culkin, B. (2016) *Postscript on Boxing: the human body, digital worlds, and boxing's living dead*. Create Space.

44.   Deleuze, G. (1990) Postscript on Societies of Control.*L'Autre Journal, no. 1* (May 1990)

45.   Regarding the idea of "liquid modernity," see, Bauman, Z. (2007). *Liquid times: Living in an age of uncertainty*. Cambridge: Polity Press. pgs. 1-4

46. Deleuze, G. (1990) Postscript on Societies of Control.*L'Autre Journal, no. 1* (May 1990)

47. See, Oates, J. C. (1987). *On Boxing.* Garden City, NY: Dolphin/ Doubleday.

48. Deleuze, G. (1990) Postscript on Societies of Control.*L'Autre Journal, no. 1* (May 1990)

49. Han, B. (2017). *In the swarm: digital prospects.* Cambridge, MA: The MIT Press. Kindle Edition. pgs. 45-46

50. Franklin, Seb (2015). *Control: Digitality as Cultural Logic* (Leonardo Book Series). The MIT Press. Kindle Edition. pg. 19

51. See, Bauman, Z. (2017). *A chronicle of crisis: 2011-2016.* London: Social Europe Edition. Kindle Edition. See introduction, "On Zygmunt Bauman."

52. Han, B. (2017). *Psychopolitics: Neoliberalism and new technologies of power.* London: Verso. Kindle Edition. See Chapter 2, "Smart Power."

53. Han, B. (2015). *The burnout society.* Stanford, CA: Stanford Briefs. Kindle Edition. pgs. 4-5

54. ibid.

55. See, Friedman, T. (2007) *The world is flat: a brief history of the 21st century.* New York: MacMillan. This is one of the classic books to ideologically legitimize the basic functionality of neoliberalism as a "smooth, flat surface" for global exchange and the operation of capitalism in the 21st century.

56. Han, B. (2018) *The expulsion of the other: society, perception, and communication today.* Cambridge, UK: Polity. Kindle Edition. pgs. 24-32

57. Schwarz, A. (2012, June 09). Risky Rise of the Good-Grade Pill. Retrieved from https://www.nytimes.com/2012/06/10/education/ seeking-academic-edge-teenagers-abuse-stimulants.html

58. Schwarz, A. (2015, April 19). Workers Seeking Productivity in a Pill Are Abusing A.D.H.D. Drugs. Retrieved from https://www. nytimes.com/2015/04/19/us/workers-seeking-productivity-in-a- pill-are-abusing-adhd-drugs.html

59. What Are The Long-Term Effects of Heavy Adderall Use? (n.d.). Retrieved from https://americanaddictioncenters.org/adderall/ long-term-effects/

60. Schwarz, A. (2017, December 20). Thousands of Toddlers Are Medicated for A.D.H.D., Report Finds, Raising Worries. Retrieved from https://www.nytimes.com/2014/05/17/us/among-experts- scrutiny-of-attention-disorder-diagnoses-in-2-and-3-year-olds.html

61. Berardi, F. (2017). *Futurability: the age of impotence and the horizon of possibility.* Brooklyn: Verso Books. Kindle Edition. pgs. 130-131

62. Burroughs, W. S. (1973). *Junkie.* New York: Ace Books. Prologue.

63. Sullivan, A. (2018, February 20). Americans Invented Modern Life. Now We're Using Opioids to Escape It. Retrieved from http://nymag. com/daily/intelligencer/2018/02/americas-opioid-epidemic.html

64. ibid.

65. Fisher, M. (2010). *Capitalist realism: is there no alternative?* Winchester, UK: Zero Books. Kindle Edition. pg. 4

66. Johnson, P. (1997) *A history of the American people.* New York: Harper Collins. Kindle Edition. pg. 390

67. Berry, W. (2015). *The unsettling of America: culture & agriculture.* ZULU: Counterpoint. Kindle Edition. See chapter 1, "The Unsettling of America."

68. Marx, K. *The communist manifesto.* New York: Pocket Books. pgs. 61-62

69. See, Zizek, S. (2008). *Violence.* New York: Picador.

70. McKenna, T. K. (1993). *Food of the gods: The search for the original tree of knowledge: A radical history of plants, drugs, and human evolution.* New York: Bantam Books. pg. 208

71. See, Klein, N. *The shock doctrine.* I refer here to Naomi Klein's important work where she chronicles a series of moments in the development of neoliberal styled capitalism — Chile, Argentina, Russia, Poland, the "disaster capitalism" that follows in the wake of both ecological and geopolitical crisis — that she frames as a series of "shocks," using this political and social instability to implement these neoliberal policies and programs.

72. See, Gallagher, L. (2013). *The end of the suburbs: where the American dream is moving.* New York: Portfolio/Penguin. Gallagher's text bears witness to this ongoing reversal of the role of suburbia in America. The old hope of leaving the city and moving to the safety of the suburbs — a central idea to postwar America — is no longer operative in 21st century American society.

73. Harvey, David. *A brief history of Neoliberalism.* Oxford UP, 2005. Kindle Edition. pgs. 9-19

74. Florida, R. L. (2002). *The rise of the creative class: And how it's transforming work, leisure, community and everyday life*. New York, NY: Basic Books. pgs. 41-43

75. McFarland, R. (2000). *Cocaine*. New York: Rosen Publishing.

76. Berardi, F. (2009). *The soul at work: from alienation to autonomy*. Los Angeles, CA: Semiotext(e). pgs. 166-169

77. Berardi, F. (2015). *Heroes: mass murder and suicide*. London: Verso. pg. 142

78. Fisher, E. (2010). *Media and new capitalism in the digital age: The spirit of networks*. New York, NY: Palgrave Macmillan. pgs. 3-4. Fisher comments on the inverted relationship of the state in the Fordist, industrial era versus our contemporary digital, globalized age, "During Fordism, technology discourse legitimated the interventionist welfare state, the central planning in businesses and the economy, the hierarchized corporation, and the tenured worker. However, during our contemporary, post-Fordist society, technology discourse legitimates instead the withdrawal of the state from markets, the globalization of the economy …"

79. Denvir, D. Their "compassion" is seriously flawed: Politicians care about white addicts - but still love the racist drug war. Retrieved April 11, 2017, from http://www.salon.com/2016/02/08/their_compassion_is_seriously_flawed_politicians_care_about_white_addicts_but_still_love_the_racist_drug_war/

80. There was no wave of compassion when addicts were hooked on crack. Retrieved April 1, 2016, from http://www.pbs.org/newshour/bb/there-was-no-wave-of-compassion-when-addicts-were-hooked-on-crack/.

81. ibid.

82. Interview with Jamarhl Crawford. Boston, MA. July 15, 2016.

83. See, Lemann, N. (1991). *The Promised Land: The Great Black Migration and how it changed America*. New York: A.A. Knopf.

84. Macey, B.(2018) Dopesick: dealers, doctors, and the drug company that addicted America. New York: Little, Brown and Co. See Introduction.

85. Morrell, A. (2016, March 24). The Oxycontin clan: The $14 billion newcomer to Forbes 2015 list of richest U.S. families. Retrieved January 07, 2017, from http://www.forbes.com/sites/alexmorrell/2015/07/01/the-oxycontin-clan-the-14-billion-newcomer-to-forbes-2015-list-of-richest-u-s-families/#724bacbbc0e2

86. Berardi, F. (2009). *The soul at work: from alienation to autonomy*. Los Angeles, CA: Semiotext(e). pgs. 96-98.

87. Purdue Fredrick was founded in 1892 by two doctors — John Purdue Gray and George Frederick Bingham. The Sackler brothers bought the firm in 1952, and then changing the name to Purdue Pharma.

88. Meier, B. (2003). *Pain killer: A "wonder" drug's trail of addiction and death*. Kindle Edition. Location 2095

89. ibid. Location 2175 (Kindle Edition.)

90. Meier, B. (2007, May 09). In guilty plea, OxyContin maker to pay $600 million. Retrieved January 19, 2017, from http://www.nytimes.com/2007/05/10/business/11drug-web.html

91. Hodgson, B. (2001). *In the arms of Morpheus: The tragic history of laudanum, morphine, and patent medicines.* Buffalo, NY: Firefly Books. pg.113

92. Marcovitz, H. (2018). *The opioid epidemic.* San Diego, CA: ReferencePoint Press. pgs. 12-13

93. ibid. pgs. 14-15

94. Meier, B. (2003). *Pain killer: A "wonder" drug's trail of addiction and death.* Kindle Edition. Location 3508.

95. A Facebook post from an individual in my personal network announcing their graduate school plans. I chose to cite this post because I feel it is emblematic of the now standard neoliberal position - that Capital and Capital alone has the potential to solve the world's problems.

96. Holland, C. (2018, October 25). OPIOID CRISIS: Phoenix clergy, faith leaders learn to administer Narcan. Retrieved from https://www.azfamily.com/news/opioid-crisis-phoenix-clergy-faith-leaders-learn-to-administer-narcan/article_c0a9f98c-d8a6-11e8-924b-979253a600c2.html

97. Azar, A. (2018, September 19). Trump administration making progress in fight against opioid epidemic: HHS Secretary. Retrieved from https://www.usatoday.com/story/opinion/2018/09/19/donald-trump-opioid-crisis-epidemic-addiction-nalaxone-heroine-column/1347574002/

98. See, http://joingroups.com/

99. Zamora, D (2016). *Foccault and Neoliberalism.* Cambridge: Polity. Kinde Edition. See Introduction by Daniel Zamora, "This intellectual recycling, which is the heart of capitalism's "new spirit," should lead us to question retroactively the theoretical moves made by a number of leading left-wing intellectuals in the late 1960s, particularly the often astonishing trajectories of former Maoists who converted so suddenly to the dogma of the market economy. We should also ask whether this "conversion" is even all that surprising."

100. See, Saramago, J. *Notebooks of Lanzarote.* Quoted from Wikiquote.

101. Han, B. (2018) *The expulsion of the other: society, perception, and communication today.* Cambridge, UK: Polity. Kindle Edition. pgs. 68-69

102. ibid. pg. 75

103. See lecture series "The Self Under Siege," https://www.youtube.com/watch?v=4wetwETy4u0&list=PLA34681B9BE88F5AA

104. I will refer to AA here even though I am focusing on the heroin crisis. The overwhelming majority of addicts do in fact attend AA meetings, even if they are not strictly alcoholics. And, it should also be mentioned, that Narcotics Anonymous — the mirror program for drug addiction — is based entirely on the core philosophy and 12 step program of AA.

105. See "The Big Book," *Alcoholics Anonymous.* (2001). A.A World Services. The primary narrative that chronicles the founding of AA is famously disclosed in Chapter 1 of The Big Book, "Bill's Story."

106. Glaser, G. (2018, January 10). The Irrationality of Alcoholics Anonymous. Retrieved from https://www.theatlantic.com/magazine/archive/2015/04/the-irrationality-of-alcoholics-anonymous/386255/

107. ibid.

108. ibid.

109. Zizek, S. (2016) *Against the double blackmail: refugees, terror, and other troubles with the neighbor.* London: Allen Lane. In this short work Zizek develops the idea of "the double blackmail" as the false choice between centrist neoliberal policies and the reactionary option of right wing nationalism. This is a similar situation here that the author of the passage in question is presenting.

110. Kim, T. (2018, April 11). Goldman Sachs asks in biotech research report: 'Is curing patients a sustainable business model?' Retrieved from https://www.cnbc.com/2018/04/11/goldman-asks-is-curing-patients-a-sustainable-business-model.html

111. Fisher, M. (2010). *Capitalist realism: is there no alternative?* Winchester, UK: Zero Books. Kindle Edition. pg. 37

112. See, Bauman, Z., & Donskis, L. (2013). *Moral Blindness.* Cambridge, UK: Polity. Kindle Edition.

113. See Zero Books video, "Is Trump objectively violent," https://www.youtube.com/watch?v=Dz-HvfVSpTw

114. Hari, J. "Everything you think you know about addiction is wrong." Retrieved from https://www.ted.com/talks/johann_hari_everything_you_think_you_know_about_addiction_is_wrong?language=en

115. Ebert, J. D. (2011). *The New Media Invasion: Digital technologies and the world they unmake.* Jefferson, NC: McFarland. pg. 75-77

116. See, https://www.sobergrid.com/

117. Dupuy, J. (2014) *Economy and the future: a crisis of faith.* East Lansing: Michigan State University Press. Locations 291-299.

118. See, Weible, R. (1991). *The Continuing Revolution: A history of Lowell, Massachusetts.* Lowell, MA: Lowell Historical Society.

119. Fisher, M. (2010). *Capitalist realism: is there no alternative?* Winchester, UK: Zero Books. Kindle Edition. pg. 4

120. The "12th Step," the final step in the recovery process as described by AA is, "Having had a spiritual awakening as the result of these **Steps**, we tried to carry this message to alcoholics, and to practice these principles in all our affairs."

121. *12 steps and 12 traditions.* (2005) New York: Alcoholics Anonymous World Services.

122. Berardi, F. (2017). *Futurability: the age of impotence and the horizon of possibility.* Brooklyn: Verso Books. Kindle Edition. pg. 112

123. Malabou, C. (2008) *What should we do with our brain?* New York: Fordham University Press. See Chapter 2, "The Central Power in Crisis."

124. Pattani, A. (2016, October 14). The new drugs that could reverse the opioid-addiction epidemic. Retrieved from https://www.cnbc.com/2016/10/12/the-new-drugs-with-a-chance-to-reverse-the-opioid-addiction-epidemic.html

125. Žižek, S. (2012). *Less than nothing: Hegel and the shadow of dialectical materialism.* London: Verso. p.4.

126. Zizek, S. A cup of decaf reality. Retrieved from http://www.lacan.com/zizekdecaf.htm

127. Remarks by President Trump on Combatting Drug Demand and the Opioid Crisis.Retrieved from https://www.whitehouse.gov/briefings-statements/remarks-president-trump-combatting-drug-demand-opioid-crisis/

128. The Marx passage is taken from, Zizek, S. (2018) *Like a thief in broad daylight: power in the era of post humanity.* UK: Allen Lane. Kindle Edition. pg. 197

129. Passage taken from, Zizek, S. (2018) *Like a thief in broad daylight: power in the era of post humanity.* UK: Allen Lane. Kindle Edition. pg. 197

130. Passage taken from, McKenna, T. K. (1993). *Food of the gods: The search for the original tree of knowledge: A radical history of plants, drugs, and human evolution.* New York: Bantam Books. pg. 199-200

131. Macey, B.(2018) Dopesick: dealers, doctors, and the drug company that addicted America. New York: Little, Brown and Co. pg. 26

132. Quiones, S. (2016). *Dreamland: the true tale of America's opiate epidemic.* Bloomsbury Press. pgs. 304-305

133. Murakami, H. (2005) *Kafka on the shore.* New York: Vintage Books. pg. 191

134. Culkin, B. (2017) *There is no such thing as Boston: gentrification and the disappearance of a city.* Create Space. See chapter 4, "From Oxycontin to Heroin."

135. Zizek, S. *How to read Lacan*. New York: W.W. Norton & Company. pgs. 73-74

136. ibid.

137. Murakami, H. (2005) *Kafka on the shore*. New York: Vintage Books pas. 5-6

138. See, Scott, S. (2018). *Millennials and the moments that made us: A cultural history of the U.S. from 1982-present*. Winchester, UK ; Washington, USA: Zero Books.

139. Zizek, S. (2003) *The puppet and the dwarf*. Cambridge: MIT Press. pgs. 44-46

140. Berry, W. (2015) *The unsettling of America*. Berkeley, CA: Counterpoint. Locations 924-934

141. Berger, J. (2002) *The shape of a pocket*. London: Bloomsbury. pgs. 210-211

142. ibid. pg. 213.